DOMAIN o4

D1063093

PROPOSALS

SMPS
PUBLICATIONS

www.smps.org

SMPS PUBLICATIONS is an imprint of the Society for Marketing Professional Services
123 N. Pitt Street, Suite 400, Alexandria, VA 22314

703.549.6117 | www.smps.org

SMPS is a not-for-profit, professional organization established to promote research and education that advances the body of knowledge in the field of professional services marketing and develops a greater understanding of the role and value of marketing in the A/E/C industry.

Cover Photo: Steven G. Mihaylo Hall, Steven G. Mihaylo College of Business and Economics at California State University, Fullerton, Fullerton, CA.

© Paul Turang Photography / paulturang.com

Book design and layout: MilesHerndon / milesherndon.com

Domain 4: Proposals

MARKENDIUM: SMPS Body of Knowledge

Library of Congress Control Number: 2016945980

ISBN-13: 978-0-9769284-9-2 (Paperback)

ISBN-13: 978-0-9974818-0-8 (EPUB)

10 9 8 7 6 5 4 3 2 1

Published in the United States of America

First Edition | First Printing

SMPS PUBLICATIONS are available for sale on most online retailers in the U.S., U.K., Canada and Australia. Books are also available to the trade through Ingram and Amazon.com. For more information, contact info@smps.org.

Society for Marketing Professional Services

THE SOCIETY FOR MARKETING PROFESSIONAL SERVICES (SMPS) is a community of marketing and business development professionals working to secure profitable business relationships for their A/E/C companies. Through networking, business intelligence, and research, SMPS members gain a competitive advantage in positioning their firms successfully in the marketplace. SMPS offers members professional development, leadership opportunities, and marketing resources to advance their careers.

SMPS is the only organization dedicated to creating business opportunities in the A/E/C industry. Companies tap into a powerful national and regional network to form teams, secure business referrals and intelligence, and benchmark performance. SMPS was created in 1973 by a small group of professional services firm leaders who recognized the need to sharpen skills, pool resources, and work together to build their businesses.

Today, SMPS represents a dynamic network of approximately 6,700+ marketing and business development professionals from architectural, engineering, planning, interior design, construction, and specialty consulting firms located throughout the United States and Canada. The Society and its chapters benefit from the support of 3,700 design and building firms, encompassing 80 percent of the Engineering News–Record Top 500 Design Firms and Top 400 Contractors.

For more information, visit our website at:
www.smps.org

PUT THE DOMAINS TO WORK FOR YOU AND YOUR FIRM.

This comprehensive, six-book series further defines the six Domains of Practice for SMPS and the A/E/C community. Learn more at **smps.org/markendium** – and take your firm's marketing and business development efforts to the next level.

MARKENDIUM
SMPS BODY OF KNOWLEDGE

The MARKENDIUM: SMPS Body of Knowledge (BOK) is the premier go-to learning resource for the successful practice of marketing and business development in the A/E/C professions. The MARKENDIUM: BOK is not a singular publication or a catalog of ideas. It is inclusive of the contemporary knowledge necessary for thriving careers and firms in these professions and beyond.

The MARKENDIUM: BOK was curated in a collaborative way by experts in the A/E/C professions and is a compilation of existing and newly sourced content. The MARKENDIUM: BOK is built on the foundation of the six Domains of Practice identified by SMPS:

Marketing Research

Marketing Planning

Client and Business Development

Proposals

Promotional Activity

Management

Icon Legend

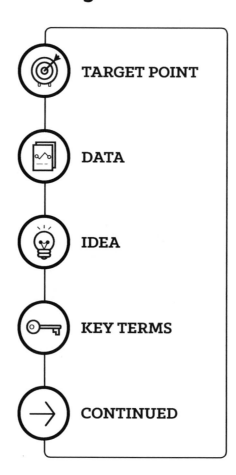

TARGET POINT

DATA

IDEA

KEY TERMS

CONTINUED

Domain 4: Proposals

Navigation Menu

PROPOSALS

Introduction

MARKENDIUM: The SMPS body of knowledge for Professional Services Marketers is classified under six Domains of Practice. These Domains of Practice are as follows:

Domain 1: Marketing Research

Marketing research is executed to gather, record, and analyze data related to marketing a firm's services. The data can be used to identify and define marketing opportunities; generate, refine, and evaluate marketing actions; monitor marketing performance; and forecast trends.

Domain 2: Marketing Planning

The marketing plan serves as a map to define a firm's market prospects and key market characteristics. The plan should include marketing goals and strategies to ensure successful direction to the team, as well as information on how marketing budgets and efforts should be spent.

Domain 3: Client and Business Development

Business development involves relationship building with current and prospective clients, often prior to a request for proposal. Through interaction with the client, development activities may include calls, visits, correspondence, social media, referrals, and tradeshows.

Domain 4: Proposals

Proposals are prepared in response to a specific solicitation where the project and scope of work are identified. Proposals can include general firm information, relevant projects, a technical project approach, and key staff résumés.

Domain 5: Promotional Activity

This undertaking includes all forms of communications and inbound/outbound marketing. Some examples include advertising, direct mail, website, social media, brochures, presentations, special events, public relations, and news releases.

Domain 6: Management

Management involves coordinating the efforts of staff and/or consultants to accomplish marketing goals and objectives. Using available resources, management effectively plans, organizes, staffs, and directs projects of an organization or firm.

As mentioned above, this fourth Domain, Proposals, covers the development of proposals in response to Requests for Proposals (RFPs). A well-prepared proposal will present the A/E/C firm as the best competitor for a particular project. In the following sections, we'll discuss how the initial go/no-go decision relies on strong team dynamics and a structured process. We'll look at the implications of a firm's going it alone, or what it means to bring in strategic partners. This section will discuss how to organize an effective response to an RFP, and put a plan in place to write the proposal.

We'll look at what you want the proposal to convey, and how to assure the client that your firm is the right firm for the job. There is also a discussion on the special requirements imposed by government proposals, and how to differentiate your firm within these constraints. We'll discuss quality control (QC) and quality assurance (QA), and then talk about how to present your proposal to the client. Next, we'll look at the importance of debriefing the proposal participants, to be better prepared for the next go-round. Finally, we'll talk about the contract negotiation process, and how fees and project relationships can be structured.

1   Prepare to Win

The first step in responding to an RFP—the go/no-go decision—relies on strong team dynamics and a structured process. You'll need to assess whether your firm can do the work on its own, or if you need to team with strategic partners.

By the end of this section, you should understand the following key points, and be able to use them throughout the process of developing, presenting, and closing your proposals:

- How to put the right decision team in place to ensure the success of a project
- How to identify the right partners and subcontractors to round out your firm's capabilities
- The importance of working with minority owned, small, disadvantaged, and other business enterprises to fulfill contract requirements and identify new business opportunities

1.1   Make a Go/No-Go Decision

A go/no-go process is a basic tool that every A/E/C firm should have and use during the initial stages of a project pursuit. Without structured evaluation criteria to help you decide which projects are truly worth pursuing, resources are taken away from pursuits that could be won and handed over to pursuits that will probably be lost because the firm lacks the appropriate qualifications to win. In order to craft a winning proposal—and particularly one that leads to a successful project—you must have a deep understanding of the following considerations well before you begin to write the first draft:

- The value the project will bring to your firm

- Which parameters most affect the successful pursuit and delivery of a project for your firm
- Whether your firm has the resources, in money and staff, to take on more work at this time
- Whether your firm has the skills and experience needed to win the project, and then to complete the work
- Any legal challenges or conflicts of interest that might affect your ability to pursue the project
- What criteria the client cares about the most (i.e., their "hot buttons")

Gathering the information necessary to make a go/no-go decision on whether to pursue a particular project or client is typically accomplished during business development (BD) efforts. See Domain 3 for a more detailed discussion on this topic. In this section, we will not go into detail on how a go/no-go decision is made, but will focus instead on how the different components involved in that decision can be applied to the development of a winning proposal strategy.

1.1.1   Build a Decision Team

The team involved in making a go/no-go decision should ideally include at least two people (and preferably more) from a variety of perspectives:

- Someone who has a strong relationship with the client, who could tell you what that client really cares about and how they prefer to be approached
- An individual who has a passion for the project and can act as the pursuit champion (perhaps the project manager)
- An operations officer or office leader—someone who holds responsibility for the successful operation of the firm, including staff availability
- A member of the marketing team who is responsible for producing responses to the Request for Qualifications (RFQ) or RFP
- A market sector leader who understands the overall market, or who is an expert in the project type

The size of the team and the person responsible for making the final go/no-go decision can change based on the size of the project. While an office leader may act as the decision- maker for a small project, a larger project whose win or loss will greatly impact the firm may require a principal or president to make the final call.

1.1.2   Understand Which Factors Affect the Success of a Project

There is a wide variety of factors that should be considered when deciding whether to pursue a project. Analyze your firm's past performance: Which factors have historically led to a successful project? What project types, sizes, and locations have been profitable in the past? In what contract types and roles does your firm shine (e.g., prime firm, joint venture, subconsultant, general engineering consultant, program manager, construction manager, general contractor, job order contractor (JOC), etc.)? Focus only on those factors that make the biggest difference in your firm's performance—trying to analyze too many elements at once can be overwhelming, and ultimately limits your ability to make a decision.

Use the following checklist of questions to explore the types of issues you should consider before pursuing a particular client or project.

Does the project fit the firm's strategic objectives?

Do you know the client?

o   Do you have sufficient time before the RFQ/RFP is released to enhance client relationships and position to win?

o   Did you know about the project before it was advertised?

Do you have the right project manager? Is the individual available?

o   Do you have the team and resources to commit to the pursuit?

o   Does the firm have the capacity to deliver if you win the work?

Is there a champion who has passion for the project and the time to commit to winning the work?

Is there time to develop a winning proposal?

Do you know who your competition is? What is your strategic position?

Are there any conditions in the RFP or contract with which you cannot comply (e.g., related to risk, insurance requirements, indemnity provisions, performance warranties, or terms that impact gross margin or the earnings ratio)?

Can you clearly differentiate your team from competitors?

Does the local office support the pursuit?

Is the project located where you can easily support it?

Do you understand the procurement process, especially the evaluation and selection criteria?

Have you vetted your project manager and other team members (partners or subconsultants) with the client?

What has been your historical performance on this type of work? With this client?

Deciding to go after a specific project should not be based on a whim or gut feeling. You should develop a rigorous process to make the decision to pursue a project as objectively as possible. Your limited marketing resources should only be used to try to win projects that support the long-term objectives of your marketing and strategic plans. See Domain 3 for more information on project evaluation processes.

 TARGET POINT

The go/no-go decision must be made fairly quickly—by the time an RFP or RFQ comes around, you typically have between two and four weeks to respond. Make sure that if the decision is to go ahead with the pursuit, you've left yourself enough time to prepare a winning proposal.

Sometimes, a firm will decide to pursue a project even when the outcome of an objective review points to a "no-go" decision. Often these exceptions are buoyed by an emotional commitment—if, for example, your team has invested a lot of time into building a relationship with a client, it can be difficult to turn down an opportunity to work with them, even if you're not fully qualified for the project. Other times, you may not know the reason a partner or principal wants to go after a risky project. There can be good reasons for overturning a "no-go" decision, but firm leadership should agree that the resource investment is acceptable given the level of risk involved. If necessary, consider elevating the discussion to a senior-level committee to evaluate the risks associated with continuing the pursuit.

1.2   Identify Firms for Teaming/Partnering

Assembling the right team can make the difference between success and failure when pursuing new markets, clients and projects, or when expanding opportunities with existing clients. Combining the resources of a multi-firm project team is an ideal method for effectively utilizing limited and, in many instances, over-committed resources. Larger staffs to draw from, combined with greater technological capabilities, can greatly enhance a team's chances of winning new projects and profitably executing the work. However, a multi-firm team requires strong project management, cultural alignment, and collaboration to enhance its ability to function as a single entity. Your decisions should create a balanced team that provides value to your client while balancing the administrative and management aspects of pursuit and delivery. There are times when self-performing the work is a perfectly acceptable solution.

Evaluate the RFQ/RFP to determine what kind of expertise is required by the client. Sometimes they will specify the number of personnel that should be on a proposed project team, as well as what qualifications the team members should have. Your own understanding of the project, site, environment, and/or any relevant political situations may also suggest other areas of expertise necessary to complete the work. This could include partnering with a subconsultant who has a strong relationship with the client, if your own firm's relationship is not as developed yet. Having the right people on your side can be an important differentiator.

Evaluate your firm's strengths and weaknesses to determine what skills or capabilities you might need to bring in from the outside to augment your team's qualifications. For example, if a vocal faction of a city's population is opposed to the project, it might be worth bringing in a community outreach specialist. For a concert hall project, an acoustics engineer would bring valuable knowledge to your team.

The formation of a successful team is contingent upon a number of factors that should have been taken into account during BD efforts. These include the implementation of effective intelligence-gathering methodologies, database development/maintenance, taking advantage of professional and personal networks, and the quantitative-based analysis of potential teaming options and opportunities. Intangible factors such as team chemistry and the development of a culture compatible with the prospective client's goals and expectations are even more critical.

IDEA

Don't overlook your direct competitors during your search for a partnership—teaming with them can eliminate one competitor and strengthen your combined team.

Once you've found a team that fits all of your criteria, consider the exclusivity of the arrangement. Prime or lead consultants understandably seek an exclusive arrangement with associate firms and consultants, especially when the consultant's expertise or relationship with a potential client will provide a competitive advantage. Locking a desired firm into your team ensures that your team has their full attention and commitment to the pursuit. Consultants, subconsultants, and associate firms that receive a large percentage of the fee are also viewed as prime candidates for an exclusive partnership strictly because of financial considerations.

On the other hand, firms that normally work in a subconsulting capacity or provide specialty services have legitimate and valid reasons for not granting exclusives. The potential for jeopardizing existing relationships with other firms the consultant has had a long-term and profitable working relationship with is usually at the top of the list. If a company you want to partner with is reluctant to sign an exclusive agreement, try to limit their ability to participate in your firm's differentiating discussions to avoid the possibility of information reaching your competitors.

1.2.1   Affirmative Action Opportunities

Minority, small, and disadvantaged business enterprise utilization goals have been established to assist disadvantaged businesses in obtaining a fair share of design and construction dollars, and are a major consideration in the team-building process. Most public opportunities require some level of participation by MBE firms (Minority-owned Business Enterprise), WBE firms (Women-owned Business Enterprise), SBE firms (Small Business Enterprise), and/or other types of small and disadvantaged businesses (SDBEs). These participation goals, expressed as a percentage of the contract dollars awarded, are specified in the procurement documents and will differ by location and agency. Private organizations are not required by law to have established participation goals, but often do anyway.

Be sure to verify the specific requirements of a prospective client when you're building your team. Review each client's policies for participation goals and objectives, the types of firms that qualify as SDBE, whether those firms must be registered in a database (e.g., client-specific, regional certifying agency, or other), and what types

of roles they should be given in your project. Typically, SDBE firms are hired as subconsultants—engineers, landscape architects, etc.—but many jurisdictions will also allow the inclusion of vendors such as reproduction companies, printers, and paper suppliers to achieve utilization goals. Determine if participation is measured against the entire contract or only against the total professional services subcontracted.

TARGET POINT

Large projects with large subcontract teams may need to assign a subcontract manager to ensure that subconsultants are receiving work, performing to expectations, and delivering to budget and schedule.

Federal, state, and local government agencies not only have different utilization goals, but also have a variety of designations for small and disadvantaged business classifications. The Small Business Administration, the Department of Commerce, the Department of Justice, the Department of Defense, and other Federal government agencies have guidelines, regulations, and certification criteria for SDBE utilization. In most states, the Department of Transportation is an ideal resource for information about utilization goals and the various designations in their jurisdiction. State departments of transportation (or another agency within the county, city, etc.) usually have a directory of certified firms that work in their jurisdiction. Municipal and public institutional clients may also maintain databases of registered or certified firms.

A subcontracting plan is often required as part of a contract. Develop one that includes the following information:

- Methods by which you will determine participation for each SDBE firm

- Services you intend to subcontract

- Methods you will use to identify potential sources of SDBE firms (e.g., existing company source lists, industry/trade fairs, social media outreach, professional association networks, etc.)

- How you will structure procurement packages to ensure maximum participation

- How you will document the procurement process and report results

If your firm is unable to meet the SDBE participation goals for the project, the subcontracting plan may also need to include proof of a good faith effort. Show how you made small firms aware of the opportunities, create a list of interested small firms and their qualifications, and include documentation that explains why you were unable to meet your goal.

The method by which your firm is expected to track participation of SDBE firms against project goals is often included in either the procurement documents or the contract. The specific reporting documents required and frequency of the reports can be found there as well. Work with whoever manages your firm's finances to track accounts payable (the fee paid to consultants on the project) against accounts receivable (the fee received from the client). If the teaming agreement is a lump sum, track dollars as a percentage of the total fee. If it's calculated in time and materials, track SDBE labor as a percentage of total labor.

Maintain these records throughout each project, as past performance records are often required in procurement submittals. Having a record will also help you to conduct post-project reviews with your teams to determine how successful the teaming arrangement was. Could a subconsultant have been better used? What worked? What didn't? Determine how the process could be improved for future arrangements.

A number of client agencies also encourage and support a mentoring approach for SDBE firms. This is an excellent opportunity for prime consultants to work with new and growing disadvantaged businesses while, at the same time, enabling their firms to achieve client utilization goals. Smaller firms are often led by individuals who are seen as experts in specific areas, or who have significant influence and cachet in the market. They can bring technical excellence, an understanding of the client, and relationships within the owner's project management organization. Help them to get certified and set up good business practices so that they can become solid team members you can rely on time and time again. Include subconsultants in training programs offered by your firm, and include all team members in a project kick-off session to share expectations, processes, work plans, schedules, and other tools.

You may also consider participating in a more official mentor/protégé program where a large firm and an SDBE firm are paired together in a formal arrangement with time-bound goals and objectives related to helping the SDBE firm achieve their strategic goals. Such a program may be developed under the auspices of a public agency or a professional organization, and typically involves the larger firm coaching the smaller firm through BD, business management, and project management processes. Some agency programs even offer compensation to the mentor for certain activities that improve the protégé's ability to perform.

Occasionally, a mentoring relationship will develop into the teamed pursuit of a project, which both strengthens the relationship between firms and looks good for proposals in discussions about past performance. The ultimate benefit of a mentor/protégé relationship is that it provides opportunities for both firms to grow, and for the individuals involved to improve their skills and expertise.

 1.3 Key Terms

Below are the main terms covered in this section:

- Go/no-go process
- Minority-owned business enterprise (MBE)
- Women-owned business enterprise (WBE)
- Small disadvantaged business enterprise (SDBE)

2   Organize to Win

To respond effectively to an RFP, you first have to clearly identify all of the information that is being requested, and then organize your resources to provide that information in a complete and timely manner. Reuse what you can from previous proposals, and develop a timeline to create new material. The key is to create a plan and follow it through rigorously.

By the end of this section, you should understand the following key points, and be able to use them throughout the process of developing, presenting, and closing your proposals:

- The amount of time you should allocate to planning and organizing your response to an RFP

- How to create a clear work plan to ensure that all of the pieces fall into place when they need to

- How to keep track of current as well as previous efforts, to know what information is available for reuse

2.1   Read and Understand the Contents of the Request for Proposal (RFP)/Request for Qualifications (RFQ)

There are a few variations of the traditional RFP, including an RFQ, an RFI (Request for Information), an RFLOI (Request for Letter of Interest), an IFB (Invitation for Bid), and a Solicitation (most often posted online by a government agency). Design-build RFPs are becoming more and more prevalent in both the private and public sector. These are similar to other RFPs, although often more complex; they often have a longer response time frame and involve a more interactive effort between team and owner throughout the procurement process. Regardless of the RFP method, with the right approach and an understanding of the prospective client's needs, your company should be able to win the work—and if you are not selected, you will have presented well and established a positive impression for future opportunities.

RFP documents vary widely in structure, formality, and specificity, so this information can sometimes be difficult to tease out of the document. Responses to RFPs can range from a brief letter to progressively complex, multi-step responses. The level of difficulty and effort in crafting an RFP response typically is directly proportional to the complexity of the client organization's processes. For example, pursuing government projects utilizing the Standard Form 330 (SF 330) document will require meticulous attention to detail within a specified format. Those vying for these projects will need to match their staff to the firms' experience referenced in the response. This approach has become a best practice for all RFP responses. Your client wants to know that the people on your proposed team have had experience on the projects you're using to show your ability to perform the work.

Multi-phased submissions are also common. In a typical scenario, the client will issue an RFQ in the first phase and will use the information received in that submission to

narrow the field and create a short list of firms they deem most qualified to participate in the next phase. The second phase is typically a more comprehensive RFP and may ask for a more detailed project approach, schedule, fees, and/or similar technical expertise that relates directly to the client's project. The final phase may be an interview, in which the short-listed firms each give a formal presentation to the client. The important thing to remember in a multi-phased submission is to define your key message early and ensure that it resonates throughout all phases. It is important to engage your team early in this process to define a solid message that can be carried through the entire effort.

TARGET POINT

A note on fees: In a qualifications-based selection—which is required by law of any government agency—fees cannot be discussed until after the most qualified bidder has been selected. Private clients are not bound by this regulation, but often follow it. Design-build procurements usually require some submittal of fee or cost as a part of the final submittal. In almost all cases (public, private, and design-build), when fee is required, it is in a separate sealed package that is opened after firms have been ranked by Statement of Qualifications (SOQ)/proposal evaluation, so that the price does not influence the identification of the most qualified firm. It can become a negotiation point, or be used to determine "best value."

The typical RFP provides all of the information necessary to develop a response: a project description, project goals and objectives, content requirements, format requirements, evaluation criteria, selection processes, as well as many other requirements and guidelines. However, related information is not always presented together, which makes it easy to miss something. Consider using a compliance matrix to deconstruct the RFP and reorganize it so that related information is grouped together (for example, each section's content requirements ordered next to the related page limitations and evaluation criteria). A compliance matrix can also be used as a tool to track assignments and deadlines, and to track the overall progress on the proposal preparation effort.

It's ultimately up to the proposal manager to ensure that any submittal requirement, no matter how small, is clarified by the client and understood by the proposal team. Develop questions and submit any requests for clarification to your point of contact in the client's organization. Be aware that sometimes questions and answers are posted publicly, which may tip competitors to your strategy. Find out if this is the case, and, if so, be strategic: structure your question so that you get the information that you're looking for without helping out the competition.

2.2   Conduct an RFQ/RFP Strategy Session

Dedicate the first 25 percent of the time you have to respond to an RFP/RFQ to planning. That means if you have 16 days to write and submit a proposal, spend the first four on the organization and design of that proposal before beginning the writing and development stage.

It is important to get off on the right foot, and a detailed, well-defined game plan sets the tone for the entire proposal process. This is an opportunity for proposal managers to identify team member roles, communicate expectations, and set clear instructions for writing styles, templates, and internal deadlines.

Proposal generation is a highly collaborative process that must include multiple perspectives in order to develop the best strategy for designing a message and creating content. So, it is important to do what you can to facilitate this collaboration between team members.

- Assign responsibility equitably so that people can meet their deadlines
- Include subconsultants in the effort, but be cautious if they are included on other teams
- Establish a common file storage location for the team—consider SharePoint, Dropbox, or any other system where multiple people can access and change the documents
- Schedule regular check-in meetings or calls for participants to share new information, get updates on assignments, identify challenges, and develop solutions to mitigate issues

It may be worthwhile to hire a professional facilitator for the strategy session (also called the kick-off meeting), particularly if there will be a good number of participants present. This makes it easier for those who will be working on the proposal to focus on the discussion, rather than fighting to keep the discussion on track. A designated note taker is also a good idea.

IDEA

Use flip charts to capture ideas and post discussion points around the room for everyone to see during the meeting. This keeps the discussion visible throughout the session, making it easy to reference prior points or make additions to decisions. At the end of the meeting, take pictures of the notes around the room and distribute them via PDF to the attendees as a way to share the meeting information in a timely manner.

2.3   Develop a Work Plan

An organized proposal-development process should be created prior to the RFQ/RFP release so that your proposal team can begin work immediately upon a go decision. A work plan is the foundation of early, careful proposal development; it will help to produce an effective document with less need for rework. It will also help ensure that all people involved in creating the proposal understand their task assignments and deadlines. Customize a work plan form to reflect your services and how your firm assigns proposals and qualifications, and involve the entire proposal development team in the creation and designation of individual assignments. A work plan is most effective when there is shared ownership to meet deadlines.

The marketing director is typically responsible for setting up a proposal planning meeting to create a work plan. While you want to keep the meeting size reasonable, it is generally productive to invite anyone who can contribute to pursuit strategy or who will be responsible for content generation. Scale the number of people invited to the size of the procurement effort. Consider the following participants:

- Account director or BD leader
- Project manager
- Discipline or task leads
- Lead estimator, if required
- Joint venture team members, if applicable
- Proposal manager/marketing coordinator

Distribute a copy of the RFP and a proposal planning template—a sample of which is provided below—to involved staff members prior to the meeting.

Include the following items on your agenda for the proposal planning meeting:

- Discuss owner requirements.
- Discuss and list your firm's (or team's) competitive advantages.

PROPOSAL PLANNING TEMPLATE

MARKETING JOB #/NAME: _____   PRINT DATE: _____

ESTIMATE #: _____

MEETING: _____   DATE: _____

INVITEES:	NAME:	FIRM:	E-MAIL/PHONE:
Operations Officer:			
Business Development:			
Operations Director:			
Estimating:			
Design:			
Partners:			

PROPOSAL/BID

Due Date: _____   BMC Owner Contact: _____

Time: _____ ☐ A.M. ☐ P.M.   Bid Manager: _____

Lead Estimator: _____

BID TYPE:
☐ Lump Sum
☐ Lump Sum D/B
☐ Other: _____

PROPOSED CONTRACT:
☐ Standard Contract: _____
☐ Custom Contract: _____
☐ Unknown: _____
☐ Operational Group: _____

Owner: _____

Project: _____

Location: _____

A/E: _____

Figure 2.1 - Proposal Planning Template (Marketing Handbook)

Past Experience (Owner/A/E/Site?): _____

Project Funding in Place?: ☐ Yes   ☐ No

Complete Bid Work Plan - at Proposal Planning Meeting:

REVIEW GO/NO GO DECISION:

_____

_____

_____

_____

REVIEW RFP QUESTIONS AND LIST CLIENT HOT BUTTONS:

1 _____   5 _____
2 _____   6 _____
3 _____   7 _____
4 _____   8 _____

COMPETITORS:

1 _____   5 _____
2 _____   6 _____
3 _____   7 _____
4 _____   8 _____

COMPETITORS STRENGTHS & WEAKNESSES:

_____

_____

_____

DISCUSSION ABOUT SELECTION COMMITTEE MEMBERS AND THEIR AREAS OF INTEREST:

_____

_____

_____

_____

Figure 2.2 - Proposal Planning Template (Marketing Handbook)

IDENTIFICATION OF PROPOSAL CENTRAL THEME:

_____
_____
_____
_____

DISCUSS OPPORTUNITIES FOR INNOVATION AND IMPROVEMENT ON THIS PROJECT:

_____
_____
_____
_____

PROPOSAL TEXT FORMAT AND RESUME FORMAT SHOULD BE REVIEWED AND COMMUNICATED TO JV PARTNERS, IF APPLICABLE:

_____
_____
_____
_____

ASSIGNING PROPOSAL QUESTIONS TO APPROPRIATE PROJECT PERSONNEL WITH DUE DATE:

_____
_____
_____
_____

DISCUSS HOW TO RESPOND TO QUESTIONS THAT ARE IMPLIED AND DIRECTLY ASKED:

_____
_____
_____
_____

COMPANY COMPETITIVE ADVANTAGES:

_____
_____
_____
_____

IDENTIFY STRATEGY/GOALS:

_____
_____
_____
_____

Figure 2.3 - Proposal Planning Template (Marketing Handbook)

IDENTIFY ANY SPECIAL INSURANCE REQUIREMENTS WHICH NEED REVIEW:

IDENTIFY SCOPE AND APPROACH OF ANY REQUIRED ESTIMATING EFFORTS:

IS IT NECESSARY TO CREATE:

☐ Budget   ☐ Schedule   ☐ Cost Model ☐ Project Work Plan

IF GMP OR HARD DOLLAR – DETERMINE PROJECT COST:

IDENTIFY I.T. REQUIREMENTS OF THE PROJECT:

REVIEW SCHEDULE:

Construction Start:	Schedule Achievable: ☐ Yes ☐ No
Finish:	Liquidated Damages: ☐ Yes ☐ No
Duration (months):	Amount:

IDENTIFY PROJECT TEAM:

Project Management (PA/PM):	Accountant:
Superintendent:	Lead Estimator:
Engineer:	Mech Estimator:
Other:	Elec. Estimator:

Figure 2.4 - Proposal Planning Template (Marketing Handbook)

IDENTIFY UNUSUAL PROJECT CONDITIONS/RISK ITEMS: I.E. BONDING REQUIREMENTS:

1 _____
2 _____
3 _____
4 _____

IDENTIFY UNUSUAL GENERAL CONDITIONS, SUPPLEMENTAL G.C., INSURANCE OR CONTRACT ITEMS:

(copy and attach as appropriate for review)

1 _____
2 _____
3 _____
4 _____

IDENTIFY MAJOR TRADES/CRITICAL ITEMS/LONG LEAD ISSUES:

_____
_____
_____
_____

IDENTIFY MBE REQUIREMENTS/ADVANTAGES:

_____
_____
_____
_____

ANTICIPATED QUALITY LEVEL OF DOCUMENTS: ☐ High ☐ Low

ANTICIPATED CHANGES (OWNER, POOR DOCUMENTS, FIELD CONDITIONS, ETC.):

ANTICIPATED BID VALUE:

Figure 2.5 - Proposal Planning Template (Marketing Handbook)

SELF PERFORMING WORK:

ANTICIPATED VALUE OF SELF PERFORMING WORK:

_____

SELF PERFORMING WORK:

Design: _____ ☐ Yes ☐ No Lead: _____

Concrete: _____ ☐ Yes ☐ No Estimator: _____

Interiors (Drywall/Ceilings): _____ ☐ Yes ☐ No Estimator: _____

Other (Demo/Carpentry, etc.): _____ ☐ Yes ☐ No Estimator: _____

Firm Name: _____ ☐ Yes ☐ No Estimator: _____

Ideal Contracting: _____ ☐ Yes ☐ No Estimator: _____

SELECT ONE:

☐ Scenario 1 – True Teaming
☐ Scenario 2 – On Their Own

EVALUATION PROCESS

Factors to Consider, Type of Work, Resource Availability, Schedule, Shared General Conditions and Staffing Coordinated, Contigency or Fee Included in Price, Owner Preferences, Competitiveness:

☐ **Bid to Win**
☐ **Bid to Submit**
☐ **Do Not Pursue**

IDENTIFY DELIVERABLES WITH INDIVIDUAL ASSIGNMENTS AND DUE DATES:

_____

_____

_____

_____

ESTABLISH PROPOSAL FOLLOW-UP MEETINGS AND REVIEW DATE(S):

_____

_____

_____

_____

Figure 2.6 - Proposal Planning Template (Marketing Handbook)

SUBSEQUENT MEETINGS:

_____
_____
_____
_____

COMMENTS:

_____
_____
_____
_____

DISTRIBUTION:

Operations Officer:

Vice President of Project Planning:

Chief Estimator(s):

Vice President and Treasurer:

Vice President – Trade Labor:

Director of Concrete:

Director of Interiors:

Meeting Attendees:

_____

_____

_____

Other:

_____

_____

Figure 2.7 - Proposal Planning Template (Marketing Handbook)

- Discuss competitors and their strengths and weaknesses. How can you neutralize their strengths or position your team as the stronger choice?

- Determine if any business utilization (SDBEs) or affirmative action is required by the owner or a government agency, or if the use of an SDBE would give the firm a competitive advantage.

- Identify project team members, including key individuals and desirable subconsultant firms.

- Identify scope of services and approach to addressing the project—are specialty services (e.g., survey, building information modeling, environmental remediation, etc.) required?

- Identify a proposal theme.

- Review RFP content requirements and determine who will address each specific one. During the meeting, the person who is responsible for proposal production should complete the proposal work plan form (provided later in this section).

- Establish deadlines for all proposal development activities, allowing for sufficient review and editing time.

- Determine if there are unique project insurance or bonding needs that require a certificate from an insurance carrier or a letter from your bonding company.

- Review your content templates and style guides, especially if partners or subconsultants are involved.

- Firms that track marketing expenditures by project should take out a marketing job number and communicate the account number to internal participants in order to track proposal expenses.

Copies of the completed proposal work plan should be distributed to all people who are assigned proposal production tasks. The proposal coordinator/manager should update the work plan every few days and post on the collaboration site (or send it via email to proposal participants), so all can monitor progress.

After this discussion, you should be able to develop a scope of work for the proposal process, and understand more about the resources and commitment required to develop the proposal. Think about how many hours will be required for research, writing, meetings, reviews, and travel, and what other expenses, such as supplies, printing, and delivery, there will be. Coordinate with the business and operations staff to learn how your firm develops pursuit budgets and assigns work hours. Make sure that the pursuit can be completed with a reasonable cost-to-fee ratio.

A sample work plan (used by a construction firm) is provided below. Some teams find it useful to merge their proposal planning template, proposal work plan, and other tools described below into one comprehensive document so that all information is in one place.

A work plan should address all aspects of the proposal development scope, including all elements to be tracked, a schedule detailing all assignments and responsibilities, and any items required from subconsultants. Some of the tools that will help your team to manage the proposal effort are described below.

PROPOSAL WORK PLAN

PROJECT NAME: _____ DATE: _____

COMPLETED BY:: _____

RFP DISTRIBUTION LIST:

1. _____
2. _____
3. _____
4. _____

POINTS TO EMPHASIZE:

1. _____
2. _____
3. _____
4. _____

PROPOSAL/BID

Person	Task	Due Date	Complete
	Executtive summary		
	Design schedule		
	Management plan		
	Construction schedule		
	Minority inclusion plan		
	Staffing plan		
	Safety plan		
	Cost model/estimate		

JOINT VENTURE INFORMATION:

Is this project a joint venture: Yes ☐ No ☐

List of JV partner(s), percentage of contrac, phone number and contact person.

JV Name	Contact Person	Phone #	Percentage

PROPOSAL COPIES:

Total number of copies: _____
In-house: _____
Main office: _____
Client: _____

PROPOSAL DELIVERY:

☐ Federal Express
☐ Hand delivered by: _____
☐ Other: _____
☐ Operational Group: _____

Figure 2.8 - Proposal Work Plan (Marketing Handbook)

2.3.1   Develop a Schedule for Tracking Proposal Elements

The first step is to determine what elements in the development of the proposal should be scheduled and tracked. Not everything needs to be tracked—scale the tracking effort (the number of elements included, and to what level of detail) to the overall size of the proposal effort. An overly complex tracking system can mire you in details or require a dedicated person to lead the tracking effort, while one that's too simple risks losing sight of how close a proposal is to being finished as a deadline approaches. At a minimum, include all meetings and deadlines related to the development and production of the proposal, such as:

- Internal/team decisions and decision points
- Specific individual action items
- Deadlines for content development
- Deadlines for drafts/completed proposal sections
- Production and delivery activities and deadlines, including long lead order items (e.g., custom binders, tabs, packaging, etc.)

Develop a schedule that defines the date by which certain milestones—including those related to proposal production, technical research, external meetings, licensure, teaming agreements, etc.—should be achieved. Take into account how each element depends on the completion of others. Are there any items that can proceed independent of the rest? Which items must be completed first before another can proceed? Identify your "long lead" items—activities that typically require more time or outside assistance to pull together, and therefore need to be started earlier than other items. Things like business forms (insurance or bonding certificates, business registrations or professional licenses, and other items that require input or approval from firm leadership), references from past clients, custom packaging, and permission requests for site tours are not things you can rush to finish.

One of the proposal manager's main tasks is to enforce these deadlines and make sure that everyone is on track to submit the completed proposal on time. Get firm leadership support so that the manager has authority to add or change staff to meet deadlines. Is there a point in the schedule where a "no-go" decision will be made based on a lack of progress? It's rare for a proposal team to get so far behind, but this still needs to be addressed so that you don't find yourself sinking extra resources into a proposal that has no chance of representing your best work.

The following suggested action items are intended to provide a framework for a schedule that encourages timely and thorough proposal completion:

- Arrange for long lead items and/or specialized materials (e.g., bonding or banking letters, reference letters or past performance documents, logos, custom binders, printed materials such as divider tabs, etc.).
- If it's a team project, send your partner(s) the items that they need to provide or address, and request supporting logos/graphics/photos. Forward the proposal text format (e.g., section content, project description, résumé, etc.) to your team members so that they can submit material in the correct format.

- The proposal manager should review available resources (such as an internal proposal database or resource library) to develop draft responses for each RFP question.
- If necessary, conduct interviews or perform additional research to draft responses to unique RFP questions.
- Gather content being prepared by other people, edit as required to tailor the content to the project, and insert into the proposal document. Make sure that the text is complete, proofed, spell-checked, and fully responsive to the RFP questions.
- Tailor résumés to reflect the individual's experience that is most relevant to the project and demonstrates why the person is assigned to the team. Verify that the résumé title matches the organization chart position. Read through each résumé to make sure that it addresses the owner's specific experience requirements.
- Tailor selected project descriptions to reflect components that will support your team's experience. Demonstrate that key individuals and team members have experience on the projects you include.
- Cross reference project names, locations, and costs for consistency on experience list figures, résumés, or project descriptions you plan to include.
- Submit the document draft to the designated team representative(s) for review. Incorporate changes and review the revised document; re-submit for review, if required, and make any new changes. Obtain a signature(s) for the cover letter.
- Arrange for any help you need in printing, copying, collating, checking, and shipping the approved document (or uploading, in the case of an electronic submittal). Obtain final approval to submit from the project officer.
- Follow up to verify that the package was received and logged in by the owner prior to the deadline.
- Update proposal content resources, project descriptions, and résumés with any new information.
- Catalog the master proposal copy, source files, and a record PDF in the firm's proposal storage system.

We'll go into more detail on some of the above items in section 3, but for now, just understand that these tasks represent the general progression of writing a proposal and that putting them on a schedule with assigned owners will help ensure that they are completed in time.

The schedule itself can be put in any format you prefer—use whichever style works best for your team. People are typically most familiar with a calendar that shows the action items, meetings, and deadlines on a day-by-day basis. A linear spreadsheet allows you to create an overview of all items that, when displayed in a list, makes it easy to see how many days each activity is given for completion and where overlap between items occurs. Both of these formats can be created using any number of software options.

The crucial thing is to make sure that team members are able to see when their item affects another. For example, if Taylor is given until Friday to update her résumé and send it to Paul, the schedule should clearly show how a delay in receiving this information would cut into the time that Paul has to compose the résumé section of the proposal. Every item depends on the rest (some more obviously than others), and the layout of the schedule should reflect that fact.

 IDEA

Make sure that you integrate the proposal schedule with other project work plan schedules. This is more critical when there is a technical design element involved (as in a design-build delivery model, where concepts are developed prior to the award). Include the proposal efforts and deadlines in the integrated schedule that reflects all activities so that everyone is aware how their action items affect those of others, across disciplines. This has the added benefit of raising awareness of how interdependent different teams and departments really are throughout the process of winning or delivering work.

2.3.2 Develop an Overall Proposal Tracking System

First, understand what elements need to be tracked and for what reasons. Where the proposal schedule details the items to be tracked for each specific proposal, an overarching system for tracking proposals refers to tracking the status of all pursuits and proposals in the pipeline, and to maintaining an updated collection of reusable (often called "boilerplate") information. A larger proposal tracking system will therefore start much earlier in the BD process—with data regarding the discovery of leads, go/no-go decisions, teaming arrangements, and government/public relations—and continue through the ultimate result of pursuit efforts.

This allows for a view of the entire pipeline of a pursuit effort that reveals important longitudinal data about the firm's proposal history and plans with the following benefits:

- Shows overlapping pursuits, highlighting timeframes where staff will be overloaded

- Shows multiple projects being tracked within a market sector, or for a specific client

- Makes sure that a pursuit isn't neglected or forgotten

- Provides information that can be used to make a go/no-go decision for future projects, such as win rates by client, project, type, project size, project manager, role, and competition

Another item to consider tracking is proposal preparation costs. Tracking proposal preparation costs over a period of time will help your firm clearly understand the investment required to pursue a project. By comparing these costs to winning efforts, you will be able to more clearly define what types of projects your firm will win and how much that effort will cost. It will also show the costs associated with losing efforts. Creating a database with this information provides a comprehensive view of a firm's proposal costs, and can be used later as a tool in deciding whether or not pursuing a project is worth the time and effort.

Tracking and updating boilerplate information is discussed in section 5 as part of the proposal close-out process, but it can also happen throughout the proposal development process. Refer to that section for a detailed description of how to maintain and organize content.

There are many different software options for developing a tracking system, and most CRM systems include the ability to track pursuits. Integrate your pursuit tracking efforts with contracting and project delivery tracking efforts so that you're able to see when pursuit and delivery efforts overlap. For purposes of integration, it's usually best to use whatever overarching tracking system your firm already has in place. If your firm does need a new system, research your options and choose software appropriate for your firm. It doesn't really matter which one you go with, as long as you have the ability to maintain the information inside it and provide access to those who need it. Monitor software upgrades and stay as current as your firm's technology resources allow.

Determine who will maintain the system, and how often that person will be responsible for logging updates. Ideally, these updates should happen in real time (e.g., as information is learned or a milestone is met), but continued maintenance might require the involvement of the project manager to encourage participation across disciplines and departments.

Work with your team to determine the most efficient and flexible reporting formats for sharing information and status updates. You may want to develop several different formats so that reports can be tailored to specific requests—being able to sort and filter a report allows for a more focused and detailed analysis of information. Consider setting up automated distribution of a general summary report that is posted to the firm's Intranet (or some other easily accessible location that all staff frequently checks) on a regular schedule. Keep in mind that this may affect who should be given permission to view or edit the tracking system.

2.3.3 Use Templates

Developing general templates that can be adjusted to fit most proposals can streamline the writing/development process by helping authors from various departments and disciplines coordinate their efforts.

2.3.3.1 Content Templates

These are outlines that provide prompts for specific items in the RFQ/RFP. They encourage guided strategic thought and stylistic consistency across multiple authors. Consider using a template for résumés, project descriptions, and project lists. Include a style guide that defines the tone content should take, provides preferred spellings

for words or phrases that have commonly accepted alternate spellings (e.g., "email" vs "e-mail"), and specifies how to refer to firm titles and project names. The style guide can also set formatting rules regarding font, point sizes, headlines, subheadings, bullets, tables, exhibit captions, etc.

2.3.3.2 Review Process Templates

Develop a checklist that includes the "must have" requirements described in an RFP/RFQ. This document should be one or two pages long and used by an objective reviewer to ensure that everything that needs to be included in the proposal is present.

Also provide instructions for reviewers—these may be different for each level of the progress review. Let them know what to focus on (e.g., typos vs compliance issues) and how to propose changes or edits. It is helpful to remind reviewers that criticism should be coupled with a proposed solution (e.g., suggestions for how something should be rewritten or illustrated, or sources for the information).

 ## 2.4 Key Terms

Below are the main terms covered in this section:

- Request for qualifications (RFQ)
- Request for information (RFI)
- Request for proposal (RFP)
- Short list
- Statement of qualifications (SOQ)
- Compliance matrix
- Work plan
- Long lead items

3   Respond to Win

With your plan in place, you are ready to write the proposal. You want to convey to the client why your firm should be selected to do the work, while staying within the constraints imposed by the RFP. These constraints are perhaps even greater when dealing with government contracts, as we'll see. Both during the proposal creation and as a final step, you'll need to subject the proposal to a rigorous vetting process.

By the end of this section, you should understand the following key points, and be able to use them throughout the process of developing, presenting, and closing your proposals:

- How to use the proposal to tell a compelling story about your company and its people
- The ability to differentiate your firm from the competition using government response forms
- How QA and QC are essential ingredients in a winning proposal

3.1   Draft a Cover Letter

There are contrasting opinions on when the cover letter should be drafted. Should it be used as the last step to summarize the proposal, or as the first step to guide its development? In either case, it is the first thing a client will see. It is therefore a golden opportunity to make a strong first impression that highlights your firm's understanding of the client's needs and your unique ability to provide a solution. However, keep in mind that rarely is the cover letter a component of the client's formal evaluation of your proposal. Use it to set the stage, but spend your time developing the content that will be scored. (Some RFQ/RFPs limit the content of the cover letter to specific items to minimize the team's inclination to use it to deliver content.)

One approach is to capitalize on the emotional side of what the client can expect from a successful project outcome. Consider this example, written for a community college science building renovation project, which states what the client plans to achieve:

> "The purpose of the science building renovation is to provide the opportunity for students to obtain the skills necessary for today and tomorrow's employment needs. Our goal, as a Construction Manager, is to partner with your community college to deliver this vision. This proposal details how we will work to achieve project goals."

Every proposal should be tailored to the unique needs of the client and the specific project. In order to be able to do this, you must understand the client's hot buttons—the issues that drive a client to make choices or take action. Usually, hot button issues come from a place of emotion: a challenge the client has faced in the past and wants to avoid, a success they want to replicate, or a passion they want to preserve. For example, a client in the K–12 education sector may want to build a beautiful, modern school, but they also need to be careful of spending too much taxpayer money. These conflicting emotional interests provide an opportunity for you to step in and provide a welcomed solution.

Meet with the individuals who have had the most contact with the client during BD efforts to learn about the client's wants and needs. Use the information you gather to focus the opening paragraph on these needs and back it up with how your firm is going to resolve their project issues.

Consider the following rules of thumb when composing a cover letter:

- Keep it to one page and highlight only a few key points—don't try to fit in every single differentiator you've identified.

- Provide three to five bulleted reasons why your firm is different from your competition and how the client will benefit by hiring your company. This could be unique qualifications of personnel, knowledge about end-users, sustainable strategies, ideas to address project challenges, or creative bid packaging to engage local firms or save money.

- List your cell phone number in case the selection committee needs quick information to complete its decision-making process.

- Provide a believable, strong closing statement.

- Have the person with whom the client has the strongest relationship/connection sign it. This might be anyone from the president of the company to the proposed site superintendent. The person with the highest position in the company doesn't necessarily warrant their signature on a cover letter.

Throughout the writing process, continue to ask yourself one question: "So what?" Is what you're saying meaningful to the client? Develop the messages in your cover letter and proposal based on what the client will want to hear.

TARGET POINT

A cover letter can serve as an executive summary, or you can choose to have a brief cover letter and then go more in depth on your executive summary. The choice depends on the preferences of the client (if they specify an executive summary) and the amount of information you need to address.

3.2 Draft a Proposal

First, develop an outline of what information will be included in your proposal. Create the outline based on the client's RFP, and double check that it accounts for all required content. Develop your section headings and subheadings and decide where you will write about which topics. Make sure that you follow the requested format exactly. Many clients use an evaluation form that mirrors the RFP or RFQ outline. Answering the questions out of order risks the evaluator missing one of your key points.

Create a theme statement. What, precisely, are you offering to the client to help deliver their project? Among these benefits, are any unique to your firm, team, or approach?

These are your differentiators—they should be memorable and provable claims that show how your firm is different than your competitors in a way that will better serve your client's purposes. Condense the advantages of your team, your firm, and your approach into one or two sentences, and let this statement guide your writing. You also could call this your proposal's thesis. The visuals and text should all align with this theme. (More information about how to create differentiators and sell your benefits is included in section 4.)

Be sure that any boilerplate information you include is tailored to the client and the project. Firms will often create standard responses, sometimes called "content starters," that address questions or topics commonly discussed within a proposal. Standard responses provide a solid starting point—it's much easier and less time-consuming to edit and add information than it is to write something from scratch. There's no need to reinvent the wheel for each and every proposal draft. That said, care should be taken to modify the content so that it speaks to that specific client/project/group/procurement process and avoids sounding like it has been cut and pasted from a different source.

All of the items included in the proposal should be consistent in style and tone to help you communicate your message. Here are some tips for how to make some of the most common proposal components shine.

3.2.1 Tell a Story

A firm's project description sheets typically consist of the project name and location, photographs, a narrative describing the project, and a bulleted list of statistics like construction cost, completion date, and size. Rather than focusing solely on components of the project, differentiate your firm by seeking out the stories of each project. What were the specific challenges the owner faced, and how did the team address them? Show examples, through stories and statistics, of how your firm provided value, and communicate those in the narrative. In addition, take the opportunity to customize project sheets and showcase why they are included as relevant experience. For example, use a call-out box to draw attention to common attributes between the project you're pursuing and the project you're featuring. You might also discuss how key members of your proposed team contributed to the success of the described project. This provides the reviewer with confidence that the experts on your team learned from the projects you show as your most relevant experience.

3.2.2 Spotlight Your Experts

A firm's résumés often include a short narrative, a list of relevant projects, education, and registration information. As with project descriptions, when including résumés, think about why each person was selected for the team and highlight that information. If members of your team have been published or have presented on relevant topics, including these items on their résumés can add credibility and showcase their thought leadership. Customize the list of projects that they have worked on to be relevant to the current pursuit; including a brief statement as to why certain projects were included adds even more customization and relevance.

3.2.3 Use Graphics

Effective use of photography and graphic illustration can be a very powerful tool in support of your message. Consider whether graphics used in past proposals can be revised or recycled for this one. It is worthwhile to create a storage system or database of previous graphics for this reason. Any time you can use a graph, chart, or infographic to deliver your message, do so. Graphics are better than text for describing complicated sets of data in a clear and concise fashion.

Let's say that a client wants you to evaluate your capacity to complete the work in the desired timeframe. They might ask you to list all of the contracts you currently hold in a particular market sector, along with the timeline of each project. You could use a list or table to display this information, but that would require close inspection and thought for a reader to understand. A bar chart that visually depicts the overlap in timeframe enables you to demonstrate that current contracts will wind down prior to this one starting up, getting the point across much quicker. Familiarize yourself with the types of charts and graphics you and others have used so that you can choose the one most appropriate for the information you have and the point you want to make.

That said, unnecessary graphics—or simply too many on one page—can confuse your message rather than clarify it. Only use graphics that make a specific point and are essential to the proposal text. Here are some tips for making sure that the graphics you do have are visually appealing and enhance, rather than distract from, the text.

- Use the same scale for all charts.
- Make sure that the terms used in the graphics are the same as those in the text.
- Number tables and graphs consistently throughout your proposal. Use those numbers (e.g., Figure 1a) to refer to the graphics in your text so that the reader can easily find them.
- Include a strong caption for every graphic (e.g., photograph, illustration, chart, table, etc.). This provides additional opportunities to prove your point and highlight a benefit to the owner.

Software makes it easy to incorporate graphics, quotes, photography, and other illustrations into marketing material. Take advantage of software and incorporate visuals where appropriate to enhance your message to the owner.

 DATA
Research conducted at the University of Minnesota has proven that pictures and graphics help increase reader retention by 300 percent.

While a picture may be worth a thousand words, including them is only helpful if they are of good quality and relevant to your message. As an example, an educational facility owner would probably not find photos of your industrial or commercial projects as useful in their decision-making process as they would photos documenting current classroom environments. Visuals allow you to "show" instead of "tell." Avoid sweeping generalities like, "Our team brings extensive experience to the project." Instead, show your experience by including photos of similar projects, and bullet the benefits you brought to the client.

3.2.4   Use Direct and Concise Language

Increasingly, clients are requesting in their RFPs that respondents write simply and clearly, with minimal text. Many selection committees have to sift through dozens of proposals to select a winning firm. Make your client's job easier by writing with clarity, following consistent rules for style and grammar, and using these tips:

- **Use the active voice.** Design, project, and construction management are active efforts, and this should be reflected in your writing.

- **Be specific and omit needless words.** A sentence such as, "We have no doubt that, because of our extensive years of experience with this type of project, Company ABC will be able to complete your project in an expeditious manner that can satisfy all involved parties," could instead read, "ABC's successful delivery of five projects with complexity similar to yours demonstrates that we have the processes in place to achieve your desired opening date."

- **Eliminate redundant adjectives.** Words such as "absolutely" and "final" are often extraneous whenever they precede another adjective. For example, a project is not absolutely complete; it is complete.

- **Avoid complex terminology or stilted legal language.** Some of the reviewers may not have a technical background.

- **Avoid loaded language.** "Loaded" language has connotations beyond its intended meaning. Some examples are misused buzzwords and words with legal implications, such as "ensure" and "guarantee."

- **Keep ideas and items parallel.** In lists and in paragraphs, keep words parallel. For example, the sentence, "This phase will include organizing, reviewing, and assessment of client data," should read, "This phase will include organizing, reviewing, and assessing client data."

- **Use bold and italics sparingly.** Bolding and italicizing text draws attention to phrases and ideas (or names), and can be very effective. However, bold or italicized text becomes meaningless when overused. As a rule, only bold one phrase or term per paragraph. If you find you need to bold two or three passages, consider breaking up the text into separate paragraphs.

- **Be consistent.** Writing that drifts from one tone to another is difficult to read, let alone understand. Find a tone that suits your ideas and stick to it. If you are compiling copy written by different authors, make sure that the final text has a consistent tone. For example, if the executive summary has a conversational tone, perhaps where you refer to your team members by first names, the rest of the document should be equally casual.

Make sure that you finish the draft (complete with graphics and full content) with enough time left for a thorough review process, as described in section 5.

3.3   Complete Government Forms

The Federal government has adopted the use of standard forms to aid in selecting firms for architecture or engineering services. In order to win work with the Federal government, marketers must not only know how to fill out the form, but also how to "sell" the unique qualifications of the firm within the boundaries of the form.

Selection is made on the basis of one document: the SF 330. A standard format allows for easier comparison of responses to the selection criteria listed in the solicitation notice or RFP. This makes comparing credentials among firms straightforward, fair, and undistracted by extravagant presentation materials. An agency's selection board often includes registered architects, engineers, and contract specialists as well as end-users. This assigned group reviews the SF 330s and may interview the short-listed firms. Specific procedures for the control of slate and selection boards will vary from agency to agency and can be influenced by the involvement of the headquarters elements of those agencies, depending on the respective approval authorities delegated.

The SF 330 (6/2004) is the form now used by Federal agencies in the procurement of architecture and engineering services and allied professional disciplines. The form is also used by some public organizations, such as airport authorities, as a part of their proposal process. While the Standard Form 255/254 (SF 255/254) has not entirely gone away, it is typically a holdover used by public institutions and state and local government agencies. The blank SF 330 and instructions may be obtained from the General Service Administration's website. See the Related Resources section for a link.

3.3.1   Understand the Standard Form 330 (SF 330)

The SF 330 includes two separate parts. Part I is project-specific and Part II is about the offeror (also known as the prime) and its subconsultants. As with any other procurement method, a list of specific criteria is used to determine the offeror's qualifications, including past performance and the proposed team members who will perform the work. The selection board reviews the submittals and identifies the firm or team that best meets the project's needs.

The forms are available online and can be downloaded in Microsoft Word or as a fillable PDF. Most firms with resources have rebuilt the forms in a different software package (e.g., Microsoft Word, Microsoft Excel, Adobe InDesign, etc.). Many of the customized customer resource management (CRM) packages focused on the A/E/C industry have an embedded form generator that allows users to pick and choose information from the overarching system to pre-fill the form. Users can then export it to whatever software they prefer in order to change or add to the form.

TARGET POINT

However your firm decides to go about populating a standardized form, make sure that you send a template to your subconsultants so that their materials match yours. This will create a more consistent submittal that implies to the selection board a similar cohesion within your project team.

Federal procurements are posted daily on the FedBizOpps (FBO) website. (See the Related Resources section for a link.) Before responding to the solicitation, make certain that your firm is qualified to perform the work. Read the FBO announcement thoroughly to determine the services that the government is seeking. In addition to qualifications, there are several other requirements that offerors must meet to be awarded a contract by the Federal government:

- Verify that the firm's accounting system will comply with Federal government requirements.

- Establish records retention procedures (see FAR Subpart 4.7).

- Register to do business with the Federal government on the System for Award Management (SAM) (see FAR Subparts 4.11 and 4.12, and the user guides on www.sam.gov). This requirement applies to the prime firm and all consultants on the team.

- Register for socioeconomic programs if eligible (see FAR Part 19, www.sba.gov).

If your firm is awarded the contract, the SF 330 proposal becomes part of the contract as a representation of current and factual information. The named team members and subcontractors/subconsultants must be used, and any change must be approved by the contracting officer. (See FAR Part 52.244-4 Clause "Subcontractors and Outside Associates and Consultants (Architect-Engineer Services)").

Finally, remember that your standard form submission is the only chance that your firm has to make the short list. Its appearance should convey that it was organized, managed, and executed with the same care that your firm will exercise on the proposed project. If you are not short listed, request a debriefing. Most agencies will ask you to put your request in writing and will schedule a debriefing after the contract with the selected firm is negotiated.

For full and detailed instructions on how to complete the SF 330, refer to the instructions found at www.gsa.gov/forms. Below is a brief discussion of the sections in the proposal and tips for completing SF 330 Parts I and II.

3.3.1.1 Part I***

ARCHITECT/ENGINEER QUALIFICATIONS

PART I - CONTRACT SPECIFIC QUALIFICATIONS

A. CONTRACT INFORMATION

1. TITLE AND LOCATIONS (CITY AND STATE)

2. PUBLIC NOTICE DATE	3. SOLICITATION OR PROJECT NUMBER

B. ARCHITECT-ENGINEER POINT OF CONTACT

4. NAME AND TITLE

5. NAME OF FIRM

6. TELEPHONE NUMBER	7. FAX NUMBER	8. E-MAIL ADDRESS

C. PROPOSED TEAM
(COMPLETE THIS SECTION FOR THE PRIME CONTRACTOR AND ALL KEY SUBCONTRACTORS)

	(CHECK)				
	PRIME	J-V PARTNER	SUBCONTRACTOR	9. FIRM NAME	10. ADDRESS	11. ROLE IN THE THIS CONTRACT
A.				☐ CHECK IF BRANCH OFFICE		
B.				☐ CHECK IF BRANCH OFFICE		
C.				☐ CHECK IF BRANCH OFFICE		
D.				☐ CHECK IF BRANCH OFFICE		
E.				☐ CHECK IF BRANCH OFFICE		
F.				☐ CHECK IF BRANCH OFFICE		

D. ORGANIZATIONAL CHART OF PROPOSED TEAM   (ATTACHED)

Figure 4.1 - Sample Pages from the Standard Form 330, Part I (Marketing Handbook)

E. RESUMES OF KEY PERSONNEL PROPOSED FOR THIS CONTRACT
(COMPLETE ONE SECTION E FOR EACH KEY PERSON)

12. NAME	13. ROLE IN CONTRACT	14. YEARS EXPERIENCE	
		A. TOTAL	B. AT CURRENT FIRM

15. FIRM NAME AND LOCATION (CITY AND STATE)

16. EDUCATION (DEGREE AND SPECIALIZATION)	17. CURRENT PROFESSIONAL REGISTRATION (STATE AND DISCIPLINE)

18. OTHER PROFESSIONAL QUALIFICATIONS (PUBLICATIONS, ORGANIZATIONS, TRAINING, AWARDS, ETC.)

19. RELEVANT PROJECTS

	(1) TITLE AND LOCATION (CITY AND STATE)	(2) YEAR COMPLETED	
		PROFESSIONAL SERVICES	CONSTRUCTION (IF APPLICABLE)
A.	(3) BRIEF DESCRIPTION (BRIEF SCOPE, SIZE, COST, ETC.) AND SPECIFIC ROLE	☐ CHECK IF PROJECT PERFORMED WITH CURRENT FIRM	

	(1) TITLE AND LOCATION (CITY AND STATE)	(2) YEAR COMPLETED	
		PROFESSIONAL SERVICES	CONSTRUCTION (IF APPLICABLE)
B.	(3) BRIEF DESCRIPTION (BRIEF SCOPE, SIZE, COST, ETC.) AND SPECIFIC ROLE	☐ CHECK IF PROJECT PERFORMED WITH CURRENT FIRM	

	(1) TITLE AND LOCATION (CITY AND STATE)	(2) YEAR COMPLETED	
		PROFESSIONAL SERVICES	CONSTRUCTION (IF APPLICABLE)
C.	(3) BRIEF DESCRIPTION (BRIEF SCOPE, SIZE, COST, ETC.) AND SPECIFIC ROLE	☐ CHECK IF PROJECT PERFORMED WITH CURRENT FIRM	

	(1) TITLE AND LOCATION (CITY AND STATE)	(2) YEAR COMPLETED	
		PROFESSIONAL SERVICES	CONSTRUCTION (IF APPLICABLE)
D.	(3) BRIEF DESCRIPTION (BRIEF SCOPE, SIZE, COST, ETC.) AND SPECIFIC ROLE	☐ CHECK IF PROJECT PERFORMED WITH CURRENT FIRM	

	(1) TITLE AND LOCATION (CITY AND STATE)	(2) YEAR COMPLETED	
		PROFESSIONAL SERVICES	CONSTRUCTION (IF APPLICABLE)
E.	(3) BRIEF DESCRIPTION (BRIEF SCOPE, SIZE, COST, ETC.) AND SPECIFIC ROLE	☐ CHECK IF PROJECT PERFORMED WITH CURRENT FIRM	

Figure 4.2 - Sample SF 330 Part I Section E: Resumes of key personnel proposed for this contract

QUALIFICATIONS/EXAMPLE PROJECTS

EXAMPLE PROJECTS WHICH BEST ILLUSTRATE PROPOSED TEAM'S QUALIFICATIONS FOR THIS CONTRACT.
(Present as many projects as requested by the agency, or 10 projects, if not specified. Complete the section below for each project.)

EXAMPLE PROJECT KEY NUMBER:

TITLE:	YEAR COMPLETED	
	PROFESSIONAL SERVICES	CONSTRUCTION *(if applicable)*
LOCATION: *(city and state)*		

PROJECT OWNER'S INFORMATION

PROJECT NAME:	POINT OF CONTACT NAME:
	POINT OF CONTACT PHONE NUMBER:

BRIEF DESCRIPTION OF PROJECT AND RELEVANCE TO THIS CONTRACT *(include scope, size and cost.)*:

FIRMS INVOLVED WITH THIS PROJECT

FIRM NAME:	FIRM LOCATION: *(city and state)*	ROLE:
FIRM NAME:	FIRM LOCATION: *(city and state)*	ROLE:
FIRM NAME:	FIRM LOCATION: *(city and state)*	ROLE:
FIRM NAME:	FIRM LOCATION: *(city and state)*	ROLE:
FIRM NAME:	FIRM LOCATION: *(city and state)*	ROLE:

Figure 4.3 - SF 330 Part I Section F: Example Projects which best illustrate proposed team's qualifications for this contract

ADDITIONAL INFORMATION

Provide any additional information requested by the agency. Attach additional sheets as needed.

_____

_____

_____

_____

_____

_____

_____

_____

_____

_____

AUTHORIZED REPRESENTATIVE

THE FOREGOING IS A STATEMENT OF FACTS.

NAME & TITLE:		
SIGNATURE:	DATE:	

Figure 4.4 - SF 330 Part I Section H: Additional Information Section I: Authorized Representative

Section A: Contract Information

- The blocks in this section identify the specific solicitation to which you are responding. The solicitation number often begins with a combination of letters representing the advertising agency. It is the unique identifier for the solicitation and distinguishes it from other solicitations with the same name.

- Enter the title and location as it appears in the notice—not the location of the contracting office or where submittals should be delivered.

Section B: Architect-Engineer Point of Contact

- Provide information for a representative of the prime contractor or joint venture that the agency can contact for additional information. This should be someone familiar with the submittal and who is able to speak for the team or joint venture on policy and contractual matters.

- Name of Firm is the legal name of the firm or joint venture.

- Make sure that the contact information is accurate and that phone and email will be answered or monitored by someone who can reach the individual, in case the firm is asked to participate in an interview on short notice.

Section C: Proposed Team

- This section discloses the contractual relationship, name, full mailing address, and a brief description of the role of the prime and each firm that will be involved in performance of this contract.

- List the prime contractor or joint venture partners first. If a firm has branch offices, indicate each individual branch office that will have a key role on the team, listing the office that will manage the contract first.

- If you include an individual on the Section D organization chart or that person's résumé in Section E, then the office from which that person works should be listed in Section C as a member of the team, and a Part II must also be provided for that office.

Section D: Organization Chart

- Present an organization chart of the proposed team showing the names and roles of all key personnel listed in Section E and the firm they are associated with, as listed in Section C.

- Clearly show lines of authority.

- The organization chart should also illustrate that you have included the required number of professionals in all of the required disciplines.

Section E: Résumés of Key Personnel Proposed for This Contract

- Complete this section for each key person who will participate in this contract.

- When selecting the team, keep in mind that, later in Section G, these individuals will need to show that they have worked together as a team before and that they have worked on as many of the example projects as possible.

- Provide information on up to five projects in which the person had a significant role that demonstrates the person's capability relevant to their proposed role in this contract. These projects do not have to include projects presented in Section F if the person worked on other projects that were more relevant than the team projects in Section F. Instead of just describing the project example, describe the person's experience on the project.

Section F: Example Projects Which Best Illustrate Proposed Team's Qualifications for This Contract

- Projects in this section should be similar in scope and magnitude to the proposed project and may include a combination of projects completed by the prime and major subconsultants. Provide a clear statement of relevance in addition to describing the projects' scope, size, and cost. The more similar the example projects are to the proposed project, the better.

- Select projects on which multiple team members worked together, if possible.

- Complete one Section F page for each project. Present 10 projects that represent the best experience of the team (whether completed by prime or subconsultants), unless otherwise specified in the solicitation.

- Include any other information requested by the agency for each example project. Consider including information on any challenges, actions taken, and results that were achieved for that project, such as time or cost savings or any innovative solutions. The project examples then become "proofs" that demonstrate where your firm has delivered client value.

- For a brand new firm, similar projects from the portfolios of the principals can be shown. In this case, it is essential to note that the contract holder was another firm.

Section G: Key Personnel Participation in Example Projects

- The matrix below is intended to graphically depict which key personnel identified in Section E worked on the example projects listed in Section F. The intent of the form is to demonstrate that the person worked on that project in a role similar to the one they will provide for the proposed contract. It is a good idea to verify with the agency how they will review this form; some may allow you to mark an X regardless of the role the individual fulfilled on the project.

- List everyone for whom you include a Section E résumé. It is not expected that everyone will have worked on each project, but more Xs demonstrates that not only does your team provide qualified personnel, but that these individuals can work together as a team to execute work.

G. KEY PERSONNEL PARTICIPATION IN EXAMPLE PROJECTS

26. NAMES OF KEY PERSONNEL (Form Section E, Block 12)	27. ROLE IN THIS CONTRACT (Form Section E, Block 13)	28. EXAMPLE PROJECTS LISTED IN SECTION F (Fill in "Example Projects Key" section below, before completing table. Place "X" under project key number for project participation same or similar role.)									
		1	2	3	4	5	6	7	8	9	10
Joe Expert, PE	Program Manager	X	X		X		X				
Nancy Specialist, AIA	Project Manager	X		X		X	X		X		X
Fred Anybody, AIA, AICP	Lead Designer		X		X	X	X	X		X	
Buddy Lane, AIA	Design Support	X	X		X	X		X	X	X	X

29. EXAMPLE PROJECT KEY

No.	TITLE OF EXAMPLE PROJECT (FROM SECTION F)	No.	TITLE OF EXAMPLE PROJECT (FROM SECTION F)
1.	Big Hangar Project, Fort Somewhere, TX	6.	Next Relevant Project
2.	Vehicle Maintenance Facility, Camp Military, AR	7.	Next Relevant Project
3.	Aircraft Weather Shelter, Air Force Base, AZ	8.	Next Relevant Project
4.	Helicopter Hangar, Home Air Force Base, NM	9.	Next Relevant Project
5.	Next Relevant Project	10.	Next Relevant Project

Figure 4.5 - Sample SF 330 Part I Section G: Key Personnel Participation in Example Projects (Marketing Handbook)

Section H: Additional Information

- Use this section to provide additional information specifically requested by the agency and to address selection criteria not covered by the information provided in Sections A–G.

- Clearly respond to the evaluation criteria, item by item. Each answer should be organized so that it is where the reviewer would expect to find it. Use headings and outline numbering.

- Use strong, positive statements in the narrative. Provide examples or proofs to backup claims made about your firm's qualifications.

- Based on what has been learned through your firm's relationship with that client, think through the benefits that your team can provide that will be of value from the client's point of view.

- On large projects with multiple requirements, incorporating an experience matrix, schedules, and other illustrations in SF 330 Part I Section H will help reviewers visualize your firm's method and approach to accomplishing the proposed project. Provide a caption for each graphic or illustration to guide the reader to the conclusion that you want them to draw from that image.

Section I: Authorized Representative

- An authorized representative of a joint venture or the prime contractor must sign and date the completed form. A lack of a signature is grounds for automatic elimination.

- Signing attests that the information provided is current and factual and that all firms on the proposed team agree to work on the project.

- As previously mentioned, the signature makes the document a legal instrument.

3.3.1.2 Part II

The second part of the SF 330 demonstrates the total overall resources of the team. As part of a complete SF 330, a Part II must be shown for every office or consultant firm listed in Part I, Section C. Take into account the following considerations when filling out this section of the form:

- Provide a separate Part II, each with its own unique DUNS number, for each office that supplies key personnel to the team.

- The Part II clarifies that firm's small business status as determined by the Small Business Administration and entered in the firm's SAM record.

- While the Part II is fact-based, it does require some strategic thinking during its preparation. When employee counts by discipline are shown, make sure that among the Part IIs from each team member, disciplines required by the solicitation are represented. For example, a count of interior designers should appear if that discipline is required by the solicitation.

- While it is not required to customize a Part II for each unique submission (signed Part IIs are good for one year; refer to FAR subpart 36.603 for details), many firms also consider relevancy when selecting which 22 experience profile codes to show for a specific opportunity. For example, a Part II submitted for a hospital job could show profile codes related to that building type (e.g., laboratories, hospitals, office buildings, research facilities, etc.) instead of railroad, rapid transit, or postal facilities.

ARCHITECT/ENGINEER QUALIFICATIONS

1. SOLICITATION # (IF ANY)

PART II-GENERAL QUALIFICATIONS
(If a firm has branch offices, complete for each specific branch office seeking work.)

2A. FIRM (OR BRANCH OFFICE) NAME				3. YEAR ESTABLISHED	4. DUNS NUMBER
2B. STREET				**5. OWNERSHIP**	
				A. TYPE	
2C. CITY	2D. STATE	2E. ZIP		B. SMALL BUSINESS STATUS	
6A. POINT OF CONTACT NAME AND TITLE				7. NAME OF FIRM (IF BLOCK 2A IS A BRANCH OFFICE)	
6B. PHONE NUMBER	6C. E-MAIL ADDRESS				
8A. FORMER FIRM NAME(S) (IF ANY)				8B. YR ESTABLISHED	8C. DUNS NUMBER

9. EMPLOYEES BY DISCIPLINE				10. PROFILE OF FIRM'S EXPERIENCE AND ANNUAL AVERAGE REVENUE FOR LAST 5 YEARS		
A. FUNCTION CODE	B. DISCIPLINE	C. NO. OF EMPLOYEES		A. PROFILE CODE	B. EXPERIENCE	C. REVENUE INDEX NUMBER (SEE BELOW)
		(1) FIRM	(2) BRANCH			
	OTHER EMPLOYEES					
	TOTAL					

11. ANNUAL AVERAGE PROFESSIONAL SERVICES REVENUES OF FIRM FOR LAST 3 YEARS (INSERT REVENUE INDEX NUMBER SHOWN AT RIGHT)		PROFESSIONAL SERVICES REVENUE INDEX NUMBER	
A. FEDERAL WORK		1. LESS THAN $100,000	6. $2 MILLION TO LESS THAN $5 MILLION
B. NON-FEDERAL WORK		2. $100,000 TO LESS THAN $250,000	7. $5 MILLION TO LESS THAN $10 MILLION
C. TOTAL WORK		3. $250,000 TO LESS THAN $500,000	8. $10 MILLION TO LESS THAN $25 MILLION
		4. $500,000 TO LESS THAN $1 MILLION	9. $25 MILLION TO LESS THAN $50 MILLION
		5. $1 MILLION TO LESS THAN $2 MILLION	10. $50 MILLION OR GREATER

AUTHORIZED REPRESENTATIVE

THE FOREGOING IS A STATEMENT OF FACTS.

NAME & TITLE:	
SIGNATURE:	DATE:

Figure 4.6 - SF 330 Part II General Qualifications (Marketing Handbook)

3.3.2 Understand the Standard Form 255/254 (SF 255/254)

As mentioned previously, the SF 255 and SF 254 are the previous versions of the SF 330, Parts I and II (respectively), and are still used by some public agencies (but not by Federal agencies). The figure below highlights the differences between the SF 330 and SF 255/254. One key difference is that the SF 330 Part I requires a matrix of key personnel and their participation in the example projects. Known as the Section G Matrix, this requirement impacts a firm's strategy for preparing the solicitation response. A team that shows significant experience working together and has developed team processes for successful project execution will be viewed more favorably by the government.

INFORMATION REQUESTED	SF 255/254	SF 330 PARTS I AND II
Landscape page orientation	X	
List of all the firm's offices	X	
List of firm's Federal contracts	X (SF 255 Item 9)	Often requested in Part I Section H
Dates for personnel degree and registrations	X	
Example firm projects, last 5 years, broken down by profile code	X (SF 254)	Summary in Part II
Count of personnel by discipline	SF 255 Item 4 and SF 254 Block 8	Reported only on Part II
Requires organization chart		X
equires matrix of people and their participation on the example projects		X
Résumés typically one page per person	X	X
Project experience on résumés limited to five projects and requires specific details		X
DUNS number for prime and sub-contractors		Part II

Figure 4.7 - Comparison of SF 255/254 and SF 330 (Marketing Handbook)***

3.3.3 Differentiate Your Firm

Make sure that you understand how these forms are being used and evaluated, and confirm that your firm can comply with all of the requirements before responding to the solicitation. Read all of the instructions closely, and respond directly to all of the information requested without saying so much that your sales message becomes obscured. Use clear and concise language. Consider how the message/proposed response will help that client achieve their goals. The most persuasive benefits or value propositions are ones that are supported by a "proof" that demonstrates where your firm has delivered similar results in the past.

Successful strategies that increase the effectiveness of your SF 330 submission focus on tying the features of your firm (the people, systems, past experience, tools, and equipment) to a specific benefit that is valued by the client. This value is a measurable experience that the client will derive from dealing with your firm that he/she won't derive from any of your competitors. For example, this can be done on each résumé in SF 330 Part I Section E Blocks 18 and 19, where you can show why each individual is not only qualified, but has special knowledge and experience to make him/her the right person for this proposed project.

Another successful strategy can be used on the Section F project pages, where the example projects can become "proofs" that demonstrate where your firm has delivered client value in the past. This value is a measurable experience that the client will derive benefits from working with your firm that he/she won't derive from any of your competitors.

In order to produce an SF 330 that delivers a strong sales message relevant to the client's needs, say "no" to boilerplate. Boilerplate is a convenient and formulaic way to fill in the boxes and respond to solicitation criteria, but will not likely persuade a selection board to select your firm over another firm that has customized their response and taken the time to understand the agency's specific project or program needs.

3.4 Develop and Implement a Quality Assurance/Quality Control (QA/QC) Process

Define the steps involved in your firm's quality processes. The QA and QC processes that your firm develops will depend greatly on the size of your firm and the scale of the project. The sample processes defined below are more suited to a larger firm with enough resources and time to conduct multiple review sessions and produce detailed guides. Adjust the suggested processes as needed to create a format that works for the scale of the pursuit and fits your firm's resources and schedule.

3.4.1.1 QA Processes and Tools

QA refers to activities related to the production of a quality product or service. These activities involve looking at the different steps in the production process and making any changes necessary to prevent nonconformities or defects in the end result. QA undertakings include training, document control, process checklists, the development of a compliance matrix and style guide, and the setting and conducting of interim document reviews.

Consider incorporating the following processes into your QA procedures:

- **Document control.** Use (or universally modify) your firm's policies for naming conventions, version control, and storage organization. Determine how email correspondence should be saved and what the format of final documents should be.

- **Proposal management.** Summarize your firm's best practices for proposal team organization, communications, scheduling, reviews, approvals, and close-out activities—think about the training and information that you would give to a new employee in your department.

 TARGET POINT

Throughout the writing process, make sure that you substantiate claims and avoid fluff. Be specific about the features and benefits of your proposal. Don't let the proposal writers get off easy without answering "Why should I care?" to each claim made throughout the submittal. Unsupported claims and clichés open the door for your competitors to impress the client with a clearer message of value.

The tools that you use should support or illustrate the "best practices" your firm has developed, and may include the following:

- Proposal team organization charts and responsibilities
- Comprehensive compliance matrices
- Typical production schedules
- Typical review agendas and instructions
- Style guides (for writing, layout, and graphics)
- Checklists and tips for various activities

3.4.1.2 QC Processes and Tools

QC refers to activities that review finished products or current service lines to ensure that they meet the quality requirements of the firm and client. The intent of this review is to identify anything that doesn't meet the defined standards, and either fix or eliminate it so that the end result conforms to specifications. QC is typically performed at the end of the line, right before the product or service is sent out the door, and includes interim document reviews, page turns/checks, proofreading, compliance reviews, and checklists.

Consider incorporating the following processes into your QC schedule:

- **Proposal team review.** Outline how the responsibility for performing objective quality checks will be divided among team members. Do this before distributing the documents for review. The content of the proposal should be compared to the client's requirements, and noncompliant or incomplete items should be highlighted for discussion with the rest of the team. Once all parts of the document have been returned with corrections made, conduct a "one voice" edit to address any differences in writing style, grammar, or spelling between parts.

- **Recovery and back-check.** Recovery refers to the processing of reviewer comments and notes. Back-check refers to ensuring that all accepted changes are correctly applied to the document and all rejected changes are explained.

- **Pre-reproduction review.** Evaluate the quality of the proposal's overall layout, including page breaks and graphic elements. Review any proofs provided by outside vendors. Make sure that all files are functional before writing them to other forms of media (e.g., a CD or thumb drive).

- **Pre-submittal review.** If the proposal will be submitted as a hard copy, conduct a page-turn review of the entire document. If you will be using an online submittal site, make sure that all files are complete and functional before uploading them.

- **Proposal progress review.** This is the most extensive and important process, and is discussed in detail below.

Proposals are expensive undertakings—it is not acceptable to lose simply because a manageable requirement was not met. Not being selected because the content of your proposal scored less than another team's is regrettable. Every proposal should go through at least one content review cycle by a carefully selected group, and should ideally have as many reviews as are necessary to ensure a high-quality final document. These proposal progress reviews are similar to the design reviews that occur during the design of a project, often when the design is at 30, 60, and 90 percent completion.

The initial review (sometimes called the "Blue Team" review) may be used to select résumés and project descriptions, and to evaluate the availability of required content. In smaller firms, this initial review is often conducted during a kick-off meeting that consists of two or three people (e.g., the principal, project manager, etc.) discussing what the client is asking for, who is available to work on the project, who would work well with the client, what projects the firm wants to show, and other considerations important to planning a proposal. At the end of this meeting, the members come out knowing what references they're going to give the client, what past projects they'll showcase, what people will be put on the project team, and what story you will tell. That information will be given to the proposal writers who will create a final document and send it out the door fairly quickly.

This more compact process is good for firms that have fewer people who need to see a proposal before it is submitted, or for those that don't have enough time or resources to go through a lengthy review process. However, this should not impact the quality of the review or submittal. If a project is worth pursuing, it is worth submitting a quality document. A pursuit loss affects the bottom line of the firm regardless of the size.

Larger firms might run through a series of subsequent reviews that systematically delve into messaging, differentiation, and compliance to ensure that the proposal continues to improve throughout the process.

The primary review (typically called the "Red Team" review) is often the only chance to catch errors before the proposal leaves your hands. In smaller firms, this may be one of the only reviews conducted, and, as such, subjects the document to an intense evaluation of all its elements at once. When time permits, or Red Team changes are significant, there may be a subsequent final review (perhaps called the "Gold Team" review) that concentrates only on catching "fatal flaws"—items that create critical quality or compliance issues.

Ultimately, the proposal is a client's first impression of your firm's ability to write, design, communicate, and produce a quality product. It doesn't matter where and when the mistake originated—at some point the proposal manager must check the numbers, verify the facts, and proofread the entire document, flipping through each and every proposal copy.

Tools that will make the QC process more efficient include:

- Proofreading tips and checklists for style consistency
- Compliance checklist (summary of requirements)
- Mock scoring sheets
- Proposal review agendas and instruction sheets

3.4.2   Determine Who Will Participate, and How

Project teams often have one person designated as the QA/QC manager, sometimes with a supporting team. A large proposal department may consider assigning someone to this role in proposals as well. Typically, an existing QA process is implemented by the proposal manager of each pursuit, or overseen by the director of the department.

QC is best performed by someone who is not intimately involved in the development of the proposal, as reviewing a completed document's quality requires objectivity and a clear perspective. This person might be another proposal manager, the marketing director, a detail-oriented person from another department, or even an outside marketing consultant. Hiring a retired member of your industry is another option, as long as they sign a confidentiality agreement.

Here are some best practices for selecting the right reviewers for your QA/QC teams:

- Reviewers should be consistent across all reviews. This avoids the potential for a redirect by someone who does not have the benefit of previous discussions and decisions.
- Choose a varied group to provide the best perspective. Include individuals who are not part of the project team.

- Appropriate individuals include any of the following (or others, as needed): the project manager, the project officer/principal in charge, the client manager, critical technical leads, a project type expert, and/or a significant subconsultant.

- Significant pursuits may also benefit from including an independent reviewer (e.g., a business consultant, or an outside market or industry expert).

- Include a review by legal counsel or a business advisor for items related to project risks.

- Consider using a facilitator for review sessions. This allows the proposal team to focus on content and capturing changes rather than having to guide the discussion. The facilitator should be either someone unaffiliated with the proposal or an outside consultant.

Consider projecting or sharing the document so that comments can be captured within full view of all participants. Before the meeting, distribute the documents to be reviewed early enough to allow participants ample time to review and develop comments and suggestions before the session. These documents should include the proposal draft, the RFP, a compliance matrix, and instructions regarding what should be reviewed (e.g., global issues vs. basic proofreading) and how to mark corrections and comments.

IDEA

It might be more efficient to request that a markup of any typographical errors, grammar corrections, rewording suggestions, and other "local" problems be submitted prior to the review session so that the meeting itself can focus only on those items that would benefit from a team discussion (i.e., "global" issues, such as a claim made without validation, or an inconsistent tone).

Again, the review process should be scaled to match the size of the project and firm—not all projects require a multi-step revision process with a formal review meeting. Take only those suggestions that work for your firm to ensure a quality submission. The length of the review session, for example, should be determined based on the size of the document and the amount of discussion desired. Small proposals can often be walked through by all reviewers together within a reasonable amount of time.

A review of larger proposals may be more efficient if the document is subdivided into sections that are then given to teams of two or three people to be reviewed separately. Make sure that the same team reviews any sections where content may overlap—this will help keep the approach to this content consistent throughout the document. Have each mini-team consolidate their comments so that one person can present the team's comments during the review session.

Whatever your approach, make sure that you allow sufficient time to address every item/issue on the agenda. A review session may need to be between six and eight hours long or even extend into a second day for significant pursuits.

Make sure that the environment is as comfortable as possible so that reviewers are not distracted. Provide beverage service, snacks, and meals if appropriate to keep the team in the room and focused on the end result. Offer periodic breaks to enable reviewers to address critical issues outside of the review room.

 ## 3.5 Key Terms

Below are the main terms covered in this section:

- Proposal
- Standard Form 330 (SF 330)
- Standard Form 255/254 (SF 255/254)
- Boilerplate
- Quality assurance (QA)
- Quality control (QC)
- Blue team review
- Red team review

4 Present to Win

Writing a winning proposal is only half the battle. If you are lucky enough to be shortlisted, you will most likely need to go in and sell your team to the client. You can make the presentation process a success by preparing the right sort of presentation for your audience, practicing until you can deliver flawlessly, and rehearsing your team to interview like professionals.

By the end of this section, you should understand the following key points, and be able to use them throughout the process of developing, presenting, and closing your proposals:

- A proposal presentation can be used to highlight solutions that differentiate you from your competition

- How to choose the right presentation media and the right team to get your message across in the most effective way possible

4.1 Develop Your Presentation/Interview Strategy

When your firm is on a client's shortlist and invited to give a presentation, the client already knows that your firm is capable of doing the project. From that shortlist, the client wants to identify the "best" firm. Doing so requires the client to discriminate, to ascertain which firm is different from the others, and to perceive benefits tied to that difference. The final phase of the client's decision process determines who they want to work with, and that emotion-based decision requires the face-to-face communication of a presentation. The team that wins will be the team doing the best job of answering the client's only real question: "Why you and not another?" They will be looking closely at how your team members interact with each other and with the audience, and whether your firm is demonstrably different (and better) from all other potential providers on the short list. In this sense, a presentation is, in large part, a personality test.

Review the client's invitation to present to figure out exactly what they hope to learn from your presentation, and how that information will be used in the selection process. Is there an agenda already in place, or can you develop your own? What are the evaluation criteria? Who will be present from the client's organization? Who are the voting members, and what can you find out about them? The goal is to discern how they are going to apply their perception of you (gained from the presentation or interview) to their decision-making process. Here are some other questions to consider:

- Is the presentation scored? If so, how (numerically or adjectively)?

- Is the score added to previous scores?

- Is the presentation meant to act as a tie breaker between you and a competitor?

If this information is not provided in the invitation to present, check the RFP. Even if you can't figure out the exact parameters of the client's scoring system, apply whatever you do learn as you begin thinking through your strategy, planning your response, and brainstorming graphics.

RFPs and invitations to make an oral presentation generally specify information to be included and requirements that must be met. Expect your best competitors to do as well as you in crafting an illustrated narrative covering the requirements. You must address every requirement to the best of your ability in the presentation. But to win, to show that you are different and better than your competitors, you must delve into the meaning behind the stated requirements.

Start by excavating the reason for each requirement. For example, 20 percent of total evaluation points may be given for a firm's "location," yet every firm has a location. What does the client want to get out of your location? Speedy responses? Taxpayer approval for keeping money and jobs within the city? Design or construction quality arising from knowledge of local substrates or subconsultants? Clients ask about features—aspects of your firm that you have, are, know, do, etc. But what they really want are benefits—the tangible or measurable things that they will get and keep that go beyond the requested requirements. Until you know what outcomes the client really desires (beyond the actual information requested), your presentation will never be able to fully satisfy the client.

Most project requirements are fairly similar (schedule, budget, safety, quality, etc.). But a client's desired benefits are always unique, because every project, as well as every decision-maker, is unique. Therefore, you can't refer to a boilerplate catalog of benefits. Demonstrate that you understand the unique aspects of the project by developing your content around the differentiators your firm has that make it uniquely able to provide the best service. Features—something your firm is, has, does, or knows—aren't discriminators unless no other direct competitor has them. Telling how your firm approaches programming, design, project management, or construction usually doesn't differentiate. While some firms have innovative labels for a task, function, or project phase, everyone in the industry does about the same activities in about the same order. Design firms don't do construction administration before conceptual design. Builders don't construct the roof before the footings. You're not giving the client a reason to select you if you're saying the same thing as everyone else, describing the same sequence or process that everyone uses.

Keep in mind that discriminators must be verifiable—they should provide clear support for the benefits your firm claims to be able to provide to the client. Take the following example: "With our firm, you have security of schedule and budget, despite unexpected events in weather, economy, or stakeholder input, because our firm—the largest in the region—has over 800 technical professionals whose expertise can be readily accessed if needed to keep your project moving forward." Here, the presenter spells out how the differentiator (the vast resources available to the firm) specifically creates the benefit gained by the client (a secure schedule and budget) in order to assuage a specific fear (unexpected events). The information that they provide is easily verifiable in a way that the non-specific claim, "Our firm is the best in library design," is not.

Identify your strategic team and hold a working strategy session. A large project may benefit from hiring a facilitator who can help you develop your strategy and rehearse the presentation. Review your proposal for the firm's differentiators, benefits to the client, unique aspects of your approach, and promises made, and consider the following questions:

- Are these points still valid?

- Are there any other points that you can make in person during the presentation or interview that weren't made in the proposal?

- What do you want the decision-makers to take away from the meeting?

Based on how you answer these questions, identify three to five benefit-discriminator pairs. Think of these pairs as the client's reasons to select your firm, and only your firm. Those benefit-discriminator pairs—with full support to enable decision-makers to understand, believe, and remember them—should form the key content of your presentation. Everything said during the presentation should support them. Here are some examples:

- "Our staff curriculum specialist constantly challenges our planners and designers to design educational spaces that are responsive to current trends."

- "By including three former DOT chief engineers on our team, we bring you experts who understand how to dissect the challenges of reconfiguring this interchange to develop a project approach that you can sell to your stakeholders."

- "Our team's history of shaving 10 percent off the schedule shows that we have efficient and effective project planning processes that will help you beat your goal to open the new facility by September 1st."

4.2   Prepare Presentation Materials

Visuals are a way to support your strategic message—they are not the message itself. Most teams are more comfortable organizing content before planning visuals; they don't know what to show until they know what to say. Without strong leadership, a team can spend precious time developing visuals that won't advance your winning strategy. Nonetheless, new approaches are often worth trying when you want to jumpstart the creative process. Remembering the "picture paints a thousand words" adage, you might have the team focus on the five major pictures that would tell the story, and then develop your presentation content to support that imagery. Just remember to balance the effort so that the team is efficient and effective.

A storyboard is a form of graphic organization that uses illustrations, images, or pages displayed in sequence for the purpose of pre-visualizing a presentation. It allows you to reconfigure and rearrange content before you begin creating the material. You don't have to be an artist to create a storyboard—you can sketch it out on a pad of paper at your desk, capture individual pages or slides from your computer, or use larger pieces of paper on a conference room wall. Stick figures are perfectly fine. Make sure to include salient points, ideas that your team has for charts and graphs, and a sketch of any graphic images that you may want to develop. Consider how the content fits the media that you plan on using. If you will be using a graphic designer or presentation specialist to develop the presentation, include them in your session so that they can understand the thought process behind the images.

TARGET POINT

The storyboard can be used to develop a detailed outline of the presentation based on your strategy. Assign a speaker for each topic, and include a time frame for how long will be spent on each section.

Review the content and storyboard with the strategic and presentation teams once they have been drafted. This review process will be similar to the one used during the outlining and writing of the proposal. Talk through the content using the outline and storyboard as a guide to see if the story flows—think of this first walk through as a preliminary rehearsal.

4.2.1   Determine the Format of Your Presentation

When it comes to visuals, match the medium to the strategy. Computer-based presentations provide great visual volume and versatility at low cost. But if one of your major selling points is the personal relationship of your project team with the client, you may want the selection panel to focus most of their attention and eye contact on the team rather than on some spectacular animation on a 52-inch screen. Similarly, if you're selling the team's cutting-edge technological advantage, you're selling against yourself if the presenters use whiteboards and easels.

The size and configuration of the space, the equipment available for your use, and the number of people in the audience will also affect how much space you have for physical displays. Boards and posters will work only if there's enough wall space to hang them all in easy-to-view locations. Easels or flip charts are more mobile and fit better into unconventional spaces. A SmartBoard is a high-tech option that allows for interactivity with the slides projected on its surface, but don't fall for the idea that high-tech presentations are always better. There's nothing wrong with a face-to-face discussion with no presentation media! A simple handout or leave-behind that helps the reviewers remember the salient points of your presentation can be enough.

Keep this handout—and any other supplemental materials you give to the reviewers—simple, short, and extremely relevant. Make sure that it supports your overarching theme or style, so it looks like part of a coordinated interview package. Here are some examples of possible leave-behind materials:

- A "placemat" that provides relevant points or graphics alongside the names of the attendees and the agenda for the presentation
- A brief booklet of information that was not provided in your proposal
- Article reprints that support your design approach or reputation
- Other usable items or keepsakes that would remind people of the value that your team provides or the personality that your team would bring to the project

When designed well and used correctly, visuals stimulate the audience's attention, understanding, and recall. The keys to effective visuals are simplicity and control so that they don't distract, confuse, or alienate decision-makers.

TARGET POINT

Determine who will create the materials (internal staff or a hired consultant?) and consider using reproduction vendors as resources for presentation ideas. Tie the pieces of your presentation together with a common color and style theme.

A good set of slides won't make a presentation, and a great topic is often hurt by bad slides. Explore the different programs out there (many offer free trials) and see what tools work best for you, your company, and, most importantly, the audiences you're trying to impress. Advances in technology have provided choices beyond the traditional Microsoft PowerPoint slideshow, and are making engaging presentations much easier to conceptualize. While it's up to you to keep up with the continually evolving presentation tools available to you, we discuss two of the current most popular options below.

4.2.1.1 Prezi

Prezi is cloud-based presentation software that allows users to zoom in and out of content at the click of a button. A free-flowing presentation (known as a Prezi) is created using a virtual canvas that can twist and tilt while zooming into specific elements.

The creators of Prezi offer a website loaded with creative templates and instructional seminars on how to compose a presentation. With its customizable format, Prezi encourages the presenter to think of a bigger picture and the overall message that needs to be delivered. One great feature of Prezi is its online platform, which makes embedding Internet-hosted videos extremely easy.

Construction firms may find Prezi useful for showcasing logistics plans, as the tool makes it easy to clearly identify where deliveries, pedestrians, and laydown might occur on a jobsite. The software allows you to create a canvas out of a high-resolution plan; its zooming feature helps you explain each area in detail.

Prezis have been criticized for featuring too much fast and constant zooming. To avoid this, presenters can instead use a pivot, sort of like ballroom dancing. Using small steps for transitioning reduces the need for larger movements or zooming from different ends of the presentation canvas. Taking the time to learn the different tools offered through Prezi can result in inspiring presentations that can make any presenter seem creative.

4.2.1.2 Interactive PDFs with Adobe InDesign

Adobe InDesign is becoming an increasingly popular software option for creating qualifications and proposal responses. Using InDesign, Adobe PDFs can be shown in presentation mode as well as easily emailed after a presentation. Marketers can take this a step further with new interactive features in Adobe InDesign that cater to today's technology.

InDesign includes a library of comprehensive, interactive tools that promote endless creative freedom. Active hyperlinks, embedded movie and sound clips, buttons, and page transitions are just a few of the features available. All of the tools are embedded into the InDesign document. When complete, the file can be exported into a PDF that's inclusive of all of its interactive features.

InDesign's best feature (especially for the A/E/C industry) is its ability to transform a submitted proposal into an entirely new canvas fit for screen presentation.

4.3   Select Personnel Based on Your Proposal Strategy

The client knows that all of the firms it short listed are qualified; they are looking for the firm that works best together as a team and is responsive to their needs. The oral presentation is the client's chance to experience your team's chemistry, and decide whether they'd like to work with you for the next few years. Capitalize on this by keeping your presentation team small and relevant—include only those individuals who will add significant value to the interview, and who you know your client will like.

When building a presentation team, your first priority is to identify the people required by the client to participate in the interview. After that, think strategically about what role an additional member could play. The only people you should bring into the room should be those who are participating in the interview, or whose knowledge is so critical to the project that they need to be in the room to answer a potential question. In addition to key members of your technical team, consider including the following people:

- A firm leader who can assure the client of the firm's commitment (e.g., a partner)
- A market specialist who can demonstrate the firm's expertise and resources available to support the project team
- A client relationship manager who will act as a liaison to ensure that the client is happy and to mediate any differences that arise
- A key subconsultant who can address a particular problem or issue faced by the client

When making your selections, consider the culture and background of the people from the client's company who will be conducting the interview. People gravitate towards people they like or can relate to. Try to bring in people whose personality types and communication styles mesh well with the interviewers', or who share similar interests or experiences. Those considerations should have been discussed when choosing the original project team. Be sure to match your client's attire as well—hopefully you know them well enough by now to know if they always wear suits, or if they opt for the more casual combination of jeans and button-down shirts.

Everyone present in the room should listen actively and carefully to the conversation to pick up on clues as to how the client feels throughout the interview. Assign one person to capture all of the questions asked, along with who asked them. Those on your team who do not have a speaking role should be tasked with watching someone on the

interview panel—take note of what that person seems interested in or bored by, if they get aggravated at any time, what questions they ask, how they react to certain people in the room, their body language, etc. Compile all observations immediately after the interview so that you have a good idea of where your team stands.

4.4 Identify Presentation Meeting Space and Equipment Needs

The more you know about the space where you'll give your presentation, the better. Most clients understand that you will want information about the room before you get there, and will be happy to answer your questions over the phone or send a picture. If possible, arrange a visit so that you can see the space in person. Some logistics to note include:

- **Dimensions.** How much space is available for presenters and material?

- **Furnishings.** How big is the conference table? Will there be enough chairs? Can you rearrange the room to suit your needs?

- **Equipment.** Does the room have built-in projection capabilities or will you need to bring your own?

- **Electrical outlets.** How many are there, and where are they located? Will you need to bring an extension cord?

- **Lighting.** Do the windows have shades? Is there a dimmer switch?

- **Connectivity.** Does it have fast Internet? Is there a phone available for a conference call in case someone from your team has to call in?

Use the information gathered to create a floor plan of the room that shows where everything will go, from the placement of presentation materials to where each team member will sit or stand. Knowing exactly what to expect makes it easy to set up even when time is short and stress levels are high.

Scope out the building itself. Where will you park? Do your team members need to register or get badges for entrance to the facility? Are there any delivery requirements? Some facilities want deliveries (including materials you carry in yourself) to be brought in via a back or side door or freight elevator. Don't let there be any surprises on the day of the meeting.

IDEA

Build a checklist for future use that includes all of the questions that you come up with regarding facilities and presentation/interview space. Update it regularly with "lessons learned."

Determine if there is any equipment that you will want to use during your presentation, and whether you will use what is provided by the client or if you should bring your materials with you. Create an equipment checklist and a backup plan in case there's an emergency. What happens if someone forgets to bring a vital piece of equipment, or if it doesn't arrive on time? What if it doesn't function properly? What happens if there is a power outage or the Internet connection fails?

TARGET POINT

Cordless

Alex and his team spent weeks preparing for an upcoming proposal interview with a targeted client. Their firm had wanted to work with this client for years, and had succeeded in positioning themselves as one of the three firms on the client's short list for a new project. Alex knew that if the interview went well, they stood a good chance of winning.

The proposal team found out everything that they could about the client's facilities and gathered all of the materials that they'd need well in advance. They decided that in order to avoid emergency technical problems, the only technology that they'd use was a laptop, and on the day of the presentation they brought two backup chargers.

When they got to the interview room and started to set up, they realized that the few outlets in the room were already being used, and the chargers were too short to reach outside of the room! They hadn't thought to bring an extension cord.

Luckily, the client was located in the middle of the city center, so Alex sent Stella out to find an office supply store. He began the interview in the meantime, improvising the introduction to make up for the lack of visuals. Stella was back in 10 minutes, connected the new extension cord to an outside plug, and they were able to continue with their presentation without too much disruption.

Key Concepts for this Story:
- As much as possible, limit your dependence on technology
- Be prepared to improvise should something go wrong
- Know that if something can go wrong, it probably will

You may have to rent larger or more expensive pieces of equipment from a vendor, and it's important to identify a reputable provider. Ask for a referral from your reproduction

provider, IT group, local subconsultant, or project team—any member of your network, really. Make sure that you allow enough time to set up a commercial account and verify invoicing/payment procedures with any new vendor.

Once you've identified a good provider, call or meet with them to discuss the following:

- Review your needs, and verify that the equipment that you're renting will meet them

- Confirm that the equipment is available when you need it

- Confirm pricing and decide how payment will be handled

- Agree on delivery and pickup times and processes

- Discuss onsite setup, breakdown, and technical support

- Ask for day-of contact information for the delivery crew and technical support personnel

Follow up with written documentation of the conversation, including all of the specifications and requirements you agreed upon. Also request a digital proof (or a hard copy, if there's time) prior to sending handouts or booklets to print, and review the proof for QC. Be careful of making any assumptions, especially when you don't have visual confirmation. A vendor's "three-ring binder" may not fit your pre-punched handouts—clarify the specific measurements/color/function/etc. of all of the materials that they're providing you with. It's easy these days to take a picture, but when you're in a rush you might just assume that they know what you want, and you might be wrong. Better to be safe than sorry.

If the meeting is far from your home office, you may have to find a vendor or designer in the local area who can rent you the equipment or create the reproductions for you to pick up when you get there. Coordinating with a remote vendor is much the same as working with someone close to home, but the margin for error is smaller and harder to mitigate. Allow extra time for back-and-forth reviews and revisions of design items, and account for local traffic patterns when arranging pickup and delivery.

4.5 Rehearse

There was a time, not long ago, when clients expected to see a firm's BD or marketing professional in an interview. Whether acting in a "master of ceremonies" role or actively engaged in the project, the person who is typically the most skilled communicator in the firm was present in this critical situation to keep things moving or to bail out others on the team who were floundering. Today, the firm's technical staff—those who will actually be doing the work day-to-day—must be front and center in most client interactions, and especially in interviews. While skilled in their respective fields, most firms' technical staff are not skilled communicators. Budget plenty of time for preparation to help them build up this skill and reduce nerves; speech textbooks suggest that, for every one minute of presentation, you should plan on one to two hours of preparation. Encourage team members to invest this time on their own parts of the presentation, prior to team rehearsals. A team that is comfortable and prepared will greatly improve the chemistry in the room.

You might not be able to dedicate such a large amount of time to preparation, but make it a goal to walk through the entire presentation at least three times with every member of the team present. Practicing the physical movements, mental connections, and logical transitions one must employ in a presentation is vital to developing confidence, teamwork, and memory. Allow the first rehearsal to take twice the amount of time allotted by the client, but by the last rehearsal, you should be able to keep strictly within the prescribed time limit. The person who monitors the time during the rehearsal should also be the monitor for the actual presentation. Develop signals that the team can use to communicate things like, "five minutes left," "stop talking," and other nonverbal messages that keep everyone on track.

The preparation room should be a safe space, free from harsh criticism and focused on the success of the individuals and the team. Record the rehearsals and use video feedback to help speakers recognize behaviors that they could improve, such as those related to posture, fidgeting, eye contact, movement, and interaction with presentation materials. Perceptions of credibility, leadership, empathy, and commitment arise at least as much from a speaker's nonverbal communication as from the content of their words. Here are three simple techniques that, with practice, can help even the most nervous presenter look poised and professional:

1. **Position your hands to move naturally.** People uncomfortable with presenting tend to either freeze or fidget. What feels and looks better is movement, especially of the hands and arms. A free range of movement requires relaxed muscles, so that movement promotes relaxation. Never let presenters hold anything–pen, pointer, note cards–in both hands. They tend to either grip tightly or fiddle constantly with it. With one or both hands empty, relaxed, and "living" in the waist-to-shirt pocket range, gestures usually occur naturally as a person speaks.

2. **Encourage full body movement.** Presenters needn't plant themselves in one location for their entire speech. They'll look and feel more relaxed if they slowly "stroll" during their presentation. Continuous pacing like a caged lion isn't appropriate, but taking three or four steps, then pausing, as they move from one content point to another is great. Physical energy transforms into vocal energy that prevents monotonous drone and adds energy and credibility to the presentation.

3. **Aim for vocal projection.** Projection is strengthened vocal velocity, not vocal volume. Projection lowers vocal pitch to enhance authoritativeness, slows vocal pace to aid clarity and attention, and "connects" with everyone in an audience to increase rapport. When you project, the air stream leaving your mouth as you speak is pushed out by an abdominal muscle–the diaphragm. But projection is controlled by aiming with your brain. In a room of any size, with any number of people present, projection will be perfect if the speaker aims their voice behind the head of the most distant person. The resulting voice will be the best that person can produce without expensive vocal training.

During the first round of rehearsals, allow each speaker to work through their content a few times with minimal interruptions. Take notes to offer feedback once they're finished. This feedback should include positive reinforcement of what they're doing well, along with suggestions for improvement—more positive statements, reduced verbosity, etc. Help them connect their content to the previous and following speakers, and develop comfortable transitions to avoid stilted hand-offs. The best way to elicit the conversational, rapport-building style that you want is to develop presentation content as a detailed bullet-point outline and have speakers flesh out the ideas in their own words.

TARGET POINT

Don't let your speakers rehearse using notes or visuals, or they will rely on them and lose credibility with the audience.

Three true rehearsals without notes are enough to tweak presentation length, adjust content gaps and overlaps, tighten hooks, smooth transitions, and embed key ideas in memory. Two more run-throughs with visuals should polish the presentation. Adjust the number and type of rehearsals to the length of the presentation and the comfort level of the team. You may, for instance, find it more effective to work one-on-one with each person and then come together for one or two joint rehearsals.

Coach your team on the proper way to interact with media and visuals:

- Stand to the side of a screen, facing the audience
- Use a pointer
- Determine whether one person will advance the slides, or whether each individual will use a remote
- If you're using an easel, practice changing boards quickly and smoothly
- If you're using a SmartBoard, train everyone in how to advance, return, enlarge, markup, and capture information
- If you're using an iPad or other interactive device, make sure that your team knows how to use it and consider every scenario or technical problem that could occur during the presentation
- Make sure that your presenters know how to use embedded links and files, and how to return from the Internet to a Microsoft PowerPoint slide

4.5.1 Conduct a Mock Interview

Figure out what you know about the client's interview team. How many people are going to be on the panel? What responsibilities do they have in the company? What have you heard about their personalities, interests, and backgrounds? Create a mock interview panel that matches the client's panel as closely as you can manage. Assign different roles to the actors on the interview team—e.g., one person is bored or focused on their phone the whole time, another has negative body language, another interrupts the speaker often—so that presenters can develop appropriate responses. If a speaker has previously had a negative experience and recovered from it, then they will be prepared to react successfully to inevitable obstacles in the actual interview. This will also serve to reduce their nervousness in the interview environment.

 IDEA

As often as possible, invite your receptionist or other administrative assistant to sit in on the interview preparation. This person is often your firm's "Director of First Impressions" so he or she is going to be hypersensitive to the jargon of an architectural, engineering, or construction professional. If something doesn't make sense to him or her, it probably won't make sense to the client either.

Provide the mock panel with a comprehensive list of questions that might be asked during the real interview. Identify the most challenging questions and focus on developing responses to them. Decide who will be responsible for answering each question, by topic. These sessions can often provide an opportunity to showcase a member of your technical team who doesn't present well. Even the most nervous presenter will often shine when asked a question about their work—how they solve a problem in the field, for instance, or why a particular part of the design plan is important. People naturally become animated and excited when they talk about their passions, and their expertise becomes apparent. If you have the time and resources available, consider hiring a public relations or crisis media relations professional to coach your team through mock Q&A sessions.

When preparing for a Q&A—whether with a coach or without—concentrate on practicing how to:

- Frame positive responses to questions
- Gain time to develop your response on the fly
- Hand-off a question
- Turn a combative question into a positive response
- Add content in your answer that was inadvertently skipped or not addressed during the presentation
- Exhibit good behavior when fielding and answering questions
- Avoid defensive answers and provide benefits instead
- Read body language
- Make sure that your answer satisfied the questioner

The purpose of the interview is to engage the client. Chemistry within your team can translate into chemistry with your audience. Creating back-and-forth conversations among team members and between your team and your audience is hugely valuable in the effort to make a connection. You want your client to get the perception that

your team works well together—show respect to the team leader, involve other members in the discussion when appropriate, and avoid the temptation to "pile on" repetitive comments that don't add new information to the discussion. With intentional rehearsals that focus on developing individual delivery, team chemistry, and natural engagement, your team will be able to demonstrate the coordination and expertise that your client is looking for.

 4.6 Key Terms

Below are the main terms covered in this section:

- Storyboard

5   Close to Win

A final, and very important, step in the proposal process is debriefing the participants, and hopefully closing the deal by negotiating a contractual agreement. Whether you have a win or a loss, it's important to understand and document the result so that you can do better the next time. And when it comes time to negotiate a contract, there is a great deal to be considered in how the relationships between the parties are structured, and how risks and fees are shared.

By the end of this section, you should understand the following key points, and be able to use them throughout the process of developing, presenting, and closing your proposals:

- How a structured debrief can give you insights into winning the next bid
- How a carefully structured contract can mitigate and share risks among all of the parties involved

5.1   Develop a Proposal Close-Out Process

5.1.1   Update Content Resources

A business must maintain current and accurate information to submit effective proposals. It is important to note that while this section is included under "close-out processes," a smaller firm with fewer resources may choose instead to include this step as part of the proposal organization process.

One person in the firm should take on this responsibility, or lead a small team to do so. This can be anyone in the firm who is detail-oriented and persistent. Having a designated person in charge of keeping up with all of the marketing information that is developed and changed during the proposal process is a worthwhile investment. Review any new content and capture changes to all standard materials the firm uses in proposals, such as the company profile, résumés, project portfolio, services, client listings, client testimonials, required documents (e.g., American Institute of Architects (AIA) forms or certificates), packaging, binding, and project approaches. Make sure that the content captured is relevant to your own firm, and not specific to the firm of another team member or subconsultant.

Photos should be added to the firm's photo library, and should be saved along with information about the photographer, the date the photo was taken, and any captions. If necessary, get the photo release and copyright release at this time. Categorize any other graphics used and add the images to the firm's graphics library, including source files.

Archive all final documents—save final PDFs of submitted proposals as well as the RFP with addenda, Q&A responses, and the list of short-listed firms. These documents may or may not become part of the project contract, but they will certainly be useful references during the project regarding the scope of effort and promises made. For this reason, include both original and redacted files.

Share final files (or appropriate sections) with all team members who will be working on the project. Distribute the information to other departments as well, including design and delivery, production, contracting, and business.

5.1.2 Organize the Files

If your firm does not have a file organization in place already—or if the one you have is in desperate need of a tune up—set up a meeting with all staff members who produce proposals and discuss various ways the information could be organized. There are many different ways information can be stored and accessed. Come to a consensus on the best possible solution for your firm. Keep the organization simple so that anyone trying to access your marketing files can do so with ease.

After a win, implement a process to capture periodic information on the project throughout its design and construction. One person should be in charge of keeping the marketing information fresh. The simplest way to achieve this is by having an information update schedule. Updates might take place monthly, quarterly, or bi-annually. Reflect on how often information changes occur within your firm and schedule accordingly. Individuals should update their résumés at least once per year. Project descriptions should be updated as milestones are achieved; once the project is complete, changes might only reflect additional services or more in-depth component descriptions. Record any other information that could later be used in award submittals.

If you're having trouble gathering current information, especially for résumés, consider talking with your principals about incorporating the gathering of this information into the annual review process. W.S. Bellows Construction Corporation in Houston, TX, conducts an audit of their marketing information annually. They identify information that needs to be updated and take the first quarter of their fiscal year to update all marketing-related information. This exercise keeps their information fresh and accurate.

TARGET POINT

There are plenty of other uses for content developed during a pursuit. Review the collected material for any mention of unique approaches, successful process implementation, or unusual collaborations that could be posted to your firm's Intranet to show the value of pursuit processes and participation. Winning proposals can be touted in a press release, or used to participate in an awards program.

5.1.3 Log Win Rates and Pursuit Costs

Keep track of your proposal record and the costs associated with the pursuit. For each submission, record the following information:

- Final status of the pursuit (short listed, won, lost)

- A list of competitors and short-listed firms, along with any scores, rankings, and other information provided by the owner
- The labor and expenses involved in the pursuit—determine the final cost by calculating the pursuit expenses as a percentage of the awarded fee
- Procurement dates and procurement processes associated with the owner
- Members of the selection committee

Tracking proposal preparation costs over a period of time will help your firm clearly understand the investment required to pursue a project. This exercise is important because firms that are not focused on tracking and understanding their internal costs do not make sound judgments about which proposals to pursue. Tracking proposal preparation costs and comparing them to winning efforts will more clearly define what types of projects your firm will win and how much that effort will cost. It will also show costs associated with losing efforts. Creating a database with this information provides a comprehensive view of a firm's proposal costs and can be used as a tool in deciding whether or not pursuing a project is worth the time and effort.

5.2   Conduct a Post-Award Debriefing

Debriefing is the act of interviewing a current or prospective client (or team member), typically to understand why your firm was not selected for a project. However, the information garnered from questions asked after a winning effort is just as important to your firm's future success.

The purpose of conducting client debriefing interviews is to understand how clients and prospective clients view the firms they hire, to learn their values and judgments, and to capture the complexities of their individual perceptions and experiences. By conducting debriefing interviews, firms develop greater client focus, enhance client satisfaction, earn a more favorable image, and in the process, learn how to improve their proposal effectiveness. Listening intently to understand the client's needs and wants more fully is one of the most important activities marketing professionals perform as a means of helping their firms succeed in today's competitive business climate.

A debriefing interview, also called a client review, is an investment in the client relationship. In these private meetings, you learn the clients' impressions of your proposals (and performance, in the case of current or past clients), as well as their perceptions of your image and reputation. When they are well planned and executed, these interviews demonstrate your sincere interest in clients/prospective clients and ensure credible technical work by removing assumptions. Professional, open interaction demonstrates your concern for and desire to better understand the client's goals and preferences, and provides you with the opportunity to create an open dialogue about how you can help them going forward. Whether the project has been won or lost, your firm will benefit from a debrief.

The critical task of the interviewer is to pose open-ended questions in a manner that encourages complete answers from the client, especially regarding expectations about

process and outcome. All marketing professionals advocate quality products and excellent service, but to achieve client satisfaction, you must allow clients to confirm their definition of quality. Based on a clearer understanding of what the client expects, you can fulfill their needs better than the competition and continue to secure ongoing business. Always approach the conversation with an open mind, and resist the urge to defend your actions or criticize what someone else did.

Clients are most receptive to debriefing interviews at their offices and at their convenience. The interviews are most effective when conducted in person, but they may take place over the phone. However, each client will have different policies and preferences surrounding the debriefing process, and it's important to understand how to best approach them within these constraints. The best time to ask a project owner about their debriefing process is during BD interactions—well before both of you are constrained by procurement policies. Many owners will address their debriefing process in the RFP, so look for it there as well, and include it in your compliance matrix activities.

Investigate the following items to learn more about a client's debriefing process:

- Is there a specific timeframe when debrief requests are accepted and conducted? Debriefs are often delayed until the contract is awarded and negotiated.

- Does the owner require a form or written request from a specific person (e.g., the lead firm's point of contact)?

- Will you get the chance to have a face-to-face meeting or a phone conversation, or do they only send a written response?

- Will they request to see your questions prior to the session?

- Is there a limit to who can attend (either to a certain number of people, or specific individuals) and/or the materials you can bring with you to the meeting? Some clients allow recording devices, while others may not let you bring anything in.

- Will the format be one-sided, where the client speaks and you listen, or will there be opportunity for an interactive discussion?

- Will you get the opportunity to view other submitted proposals?

5.2.1 Choose the Participants

The people who should attend the debrief will depend on who the interview is with from the client's organization. It may be advantageous to match participants peer to peer, and to have people present from at least two levels of your organization. This could include someone from firm leadership; a project leader; a member of the client service, BD, or proposal team; or an outside consultant. Choose at least two or three people to attend so that you can triangulate their responses post-interview to fully understand everything the client revealed.

Whatever their role, all participants must be patient and thoughtful listeners. It is critical that they remain objective and learn as much as possible from the client, which means being able to refrain from becoming defensive or trying to prove a point. It's often easier to get objective feedback by sending people who were not directly involved in the pursuit.

5.2.2   Develop Open-Ended Questions

A successful debriefing session results from determining in advance what information to elicit. The quality of the information obtained during an interview is largely dependent on the interviewer's preparation. Firms may prepare by asking:

- What is the specific purpose of this debriefing session?
- Which members of the client organization should be interviewed?
- What specifically do we want to learn?

From the answers to these questions, prepare probing follow-up questions for the client and then call to schedule the debriefing meeting. Coming to the meeting with a prepared list of questions and a notepad for writing down answers (or a recorder, if allowed) shows the clients that their responses are being taken seriously. Faced with thoughtful preparation, clients usually give questions thoughtful consideration before answering.

During the interview, maintain flexibility to be able to pursue information in whatever direction appears to be appropriate, depending on what emerges from a given response. Allow the questions to flow from the immediate context and build a conversation, rather than automatically asking the questions in order. Use the list of prepared questions to keep the interaction focused, but encourage opinions and emotions to surface. Also, use the prepared questions as a guide for listening to what is not being said. These areas should be brought up, albeit with great tact.

Phrase questions in a manner that encourages a client to talk freely. Such questions often start with "how," "what," and "where." Be careful with questions starting with "why;" they may inadvertently sound threatening. Avoid questions that may be answered with a curt "yes" or "no" or with a terse factual answer. Review the questions to ensure that the wording does not suggest an expected answer. For example, when asked, "How satisfied were you with our communication?" the client might feel limited to a modifier as an answer: "pretty satisfied," "kind of satisfied," "mostly satisfied," and so on. A better, open-ended question would be, "What is your opinion of our communication?"

Ask one question at a time and wait for a complete response before asking the next one. Be patient with the client, as pausing after a question often prompts further worthwhile information. Multiple questions may seem to be related and even efficient, but they are likely to confuse the client about what is really being asked, and confusion generates tension that interferes with frank communication. Similarly, it is the responsibility of the interviewer to make it clear to the client what is being asked. Asking questions that are understandable is an important part of establishing rapport.

Use preliminary statements to let the client know what is going to be asked before it is asked, especially when making a transition from one topic to another. For example,

"Now I'd like to ask you about our proposal organization." This serves two functions. First, it alerts the client to the nature of the question that is coming, it directs their awareness, and it focuses their attention. Second, a cue about the upcoming topic gives the client a few seconds to organize some thoughts before a question is actually asked. This technique often reduces the time spent in awkward silence as a result of an abrupt transition.

The value of the answer is often determined by the value of the question. Asking simple or meaningless questions will only elicit simple or meaningless answers. Dare to ask important questions to evoke thoughtful answers. These kinds of questions take time and thought to develop. Include a few different people in the brainstorming session and ask for their impressions or perceptions of your people, experience, and approach. Practice asking the same question in different ways—rewording or slighting changing the angle of a question may elicit a different answer. Below are some appropriate questions for each of the debriefing opportunities.

For an accepted proposal:

- How did you determine the criteria that you used to score/award this contract? Were the criteria used to score/award this contract unique, or are they used on all of your contracts?

- What were the most important criteria that you used to determine the award? How did we measure in this area(s)?

- What piece or pieces of our proposal and/or interview enabled you to learn the most information about our team, and why? Where would you have liked to hear more?

- How did you feel about our ability to communicate our ideas clearly?

- What was it about our team that made us stand out when it came time to make your decision?

- What recommendations do you have for us on future submittals? What could or should we do better or differently to make our proposals even better?

- What other RFP opportunities do you foresee in the near future? How do we get on a distribution list to make sure that we get them?

- What are your expectations for this project? Has anything changed from the RFP?

For a rejected proposal:

- May we see the winning proposal?

- What were the most important criteria that you used to determine the award? How did we measure in this area(s)? How did the winning bid measure up?

- What was different about the winning team's proposal that set them apart?

- What factors led you to believe that the firm selected will be successful?

- What pieces of our proposal/interview did you like the most/least?

- How did you feel about our ability to communicate our ideas clearly?

- What thoughts do you have on how we could have made our team/proposal stronger?
- What could we have done to receive a higher score?
- What recommendations do you have for us on future submittals? What could or should we do better or differently?

 TARGET POINT
Understand that most owners only allow you to ask questions related to your own team's performance—they often won't discuss what your competition did or didn't do. Asking the right questions can help you decode what you did that others didn't, or where and how others exceeded your score.

Throughout the interview, watch the client's body language—in particular, look out for signs of impatience, aggression, or defensiveness—and recognize when to change tack and when it's time to leave. End the session on time or early and express appreciation for the owner's time and effort.

Immediately afterwards, assemble all of the attendees together and capture as many questions, comments, responses, and perceptions that they had during the meeting as possible. Distill the comments and review them as a group to make sure that everyone agrees on the interpretations of the interview. Document the results and lessons learned, and share these with all members of the proposal team. Address any issues that the owner brought up, and follow up with them within a reasonable time frame to let them know how you have benefited from their advice, changed a process, or otherwise improved your ability to respond to them in the future. And, of course, always send a thank-you note!

While we have discussed owner client debriefs here, keep in mind that another entity could also be your client. Consider conducting a similar debrief with a major teaming partner to improve your ability to team again. Or, a marketing team might debrief the project pursuit team for ways to improve their relationship and service during a pursuit. A debrief helps the team discover what the client expects and how the client thinks. An after action review, or AAR (as described below), focuses on improving internal processes and working relationships. With extreme care and a thoughtful approach, a debrief can transition into an AAR that benefits both parties.

5.2.3   After Action Reviews (AARs)

An AAR is an open dialogue with the people involved in the project pursuit. It is helpful to conduct an AAR before a formal debrief session is held with the client. An AAR can be scaled to the situation, but is always useful as a way to organize thoughts, clear the air among team members, improve processes, and collect "lessons learned."

An AAR might discuss the following items:

- An objective description of what happened

- What went well, why it did, and how you can make sure that it happens again

- What didn't work, why it failed, and how you can prevent or improve it in the future

- What best practices were implemented or developed

- What lessons were learned, and how you can use them to develop new best practices

Consider holding several AARs, starting with smaller focus groups and gradually increasing the scope to include broader groups. For instance, the first AAR could concentrate solely on the processes and approach used by the focus team itself (e.g., the proposal team). Then, assess the interactions between the focus team and others within the firm who were involved in the pursuit (e.g., How did the proposal team and the project technical team interact?). Finally, turn the emphasis toward how the focus team interacted with those outside of the firm—for example, how they communicated with subconsultants.

The goal of starting with a smaller team is to enable them to air their complaints within a safe environment, and then switch the focus to developing suggestions for improvement that can be used to positively influence AARs with the broader groups. Disagreements or conflicts within the proposal team don't need to be dissected and resolved in front of the technical team or subconsultants. However, sharing the outcome of your smaller team discussion with those groups later could lead to an improvement that affects the broader team. It also prepares you to address that issue should it be brought up in later sessions, and gives you time to frame an aggravating situation in a way that doesn't put others on the defensive.

Document the lessons learned from all AARs and develop them into best practices for future use. Consider categorizing these lessons by topic or practice area to make them easier to implement.

5.3   Determine the Fee Structure

At the outset, it may seem like marketing and finance are two distinct and separate disciplines, but in fact they are not. In well-run, cohesive, and profitable firms, marketing and finance should be inseparable. Producing a profitable project may be heavily dependent on how well the technical staff performs their work. However, profitability can also be, at least in part, a function of the financial savvy of the marketer. This is particularly evident during the development of a fee structure.

Early in the pursuit process, hold a brainstorming session to develop a contracting strategy. Identify the value that you provide that may warrant a higher-than-market rate. Outline how you will negotiate and execute your contract, and determine the negotiations timeline. How can you shorten the time between selection and the notice to proceed? Use your relationship with your client (hopefully made strong during

BD activities!) to ask them if they will share their contract with you, if they have not already done so. If you find some terms in it that would make your firm uncomfortable signing it, go back to the owner and talk it through with them. For example, "Our experience with this kind of language is that it causes a difficult situation down the road. Would you consider modifying the language used?" While they might not be willing to completely modify it, opening communication lines might make it possible to negotiate something later that is acceptable to both parties.

If you start these steps before your team is selected for the project, you can bring in a pre-approved modified agreement that both parties are willing to sign in a short period of time. It is advantageous to both you and the client to be able to hit the ground running as soon as you are officially selected, so do all of this pre-planning ahead of time. One of the most frequent reasons for the client to shift the award to the second place firm is the inability to negotiate an acceptable agreement with the selected firm. No firm wants to lose a project in this way!

5.3.1 Understand the Types of Fee Structures Available

Unless the client already has a set fee structure in place (check their RFP, or ask), you may be able to negotiate the type that your firm prefers. Understand the options available to you so that you can make an informed decision.

 TARGET POINT
A Note on A/E vs C Firms

A construction firm is more likely than a professional services firm to bid a contract for a hard cost that includes their fees. The owner often chooses the lowest construction bid, rather than selecting a firm based on the value that they could bring them. More sophisticated construction firms try to negotiate a bid directly with the owner rather than participating in a bid war. They engage with the owner earlier in the process to have more control over the eventual price. This effort is a blend of BD and pre-construction services, sometimes an investment, sometimes compensated— as when the construction firm works with the architect and engineer to make sure that the design is viable for construction, or to suggest a more cost- or schedule-efficient change. As they help with the design, they are also working to lessen their construction costs down the road.

5.3.1.1 Lump Sum

In this fee structure, you determine a fixed fee under which you agree to deliver a specific scope of work. For lump sum contracts, it's critical to ensure that there is a mutual understanding between you and the client on the specific services being provided, described in a definitive scope of services. However, when properly used, the lump-sum contract can result in much higher profits than cost-based pricing.

Additional requests or changes by the owner must be evaluated against this pre-determined scope and fee. You can be flexible and give additional services without cost, but most times you will negotiate a change order with an additional scope and fee.

5.3.1.2 Cost Plus

For cost-plus contracts, you agree to provide services at cost plus a multiplier (e.g., 2.75). The contract may cap certain rates (e.g., engineers can be paid up to $75 an hour), and if you pay your staff more than the capped rates, your profits will be lower. This fee type requires you to think about how you staff the project, and whether you'll be able to make money given who will be assigned to the project team.

5.3.1.3 Cost Plus Fixed Fee

For cost-plus fixed-fee contracts, you agree to provide services with reimbursement at a 160 percent overhead rate with a 10 percent profit percentage (for example). This requires your firm to perform efficiently and with low overhead to maximize earnings. There may be non-billable items or services involved in delivery that reduce your profit—monitor these items carefully to mitigate their impact.

Contracts associated with FAR-adjustable projects will have to be tweaked each year to account for changes in allowable overhead rates.

5.3.1.4 Billing Rates

In this contract, you are paid based on the billing rates of your employees plus a reimbursement that includes profit. Your profit therefore increases if the people performing the work are paid at a lower rate than negotiated.

5.3.2   Research Historical Costs of Similar Projects

Research the typical scope of work for this type of project—both inside your firm and within the larger market—and use the data you collect to identify in specific terms the scope of work likely to be performed on this particular project. The more detailed the description of the scope of services, the better chance that you have of avoiding disputes concerning your services down the road. This rings particularly true with respect to changes in scope made by the owner or others to the project during the course of your work. If you have prepared a detailed scope of work, supported by estimates showing what you anticipate doing, then you will have greater leverage in obtaining additional fees for performing work that you can show is beyond the original scope.

If possible, investigate the scope of work and clarify it with the client ahead of the procurement. Get copies of professional service agreements or contracts used by the owner in the past. Remember that costs will be lower for project types where your firm has a great deal of experience, in familiar geographies where you know the competitive and delivery environments, and for clients with whom you have an existing relationship. Factor these into your total cost estimate.

In order to come up with a fee structure, you need to know what profit your firm wants to make on the project and the costs that they expect to take on. This is called the net profit ratio. The net profit ratio is the ratio of net profit (income minus expenses) to net revenues. Depending on how one's firm is structured, the net profit ratio or percentage can vary depending on one's definition of revenue. It can be based on net (before) or total (after) revenues. Pass-through items such as consultants and other reimbursable expenses, distribution of profit, bonus, and other discretionary items may be included or excluded. A firm's profit can vary, but let's all agree—it should be a positive number. The net profit ratio is calculated as follows:

 Net profit (income − expenses) / Net revenue = Net profit ratio

5.3.3 Be Able to Understand the Contract and All Obligations

Related to defining the scope of work is identifying the obligations of the design professional under the agreement. You should carefully review all activities you intend to perform during the course of a project and make sure that they are accurately reflected in the context of the agreement. Watch for items that could affect your risk, ability to turn a profit, or approach to the project contract and delivery. Such items may include:

- Conflicting or unclear language
- Undefined terms or expectations
- The contract type (lump sum, cost plus, etc.)
- Cost proposals and billable rates
- Salary caps, overhead caps, or Federal Acquisition Regulation (FAR) limits
- Limits on escalation (restrictions on salary rate increases year to year)
- Overhead rates (FAR-audited vs negotiable)
- Whether the client will pay for expenses
- Indemnity provisions
- Performance warranties
- Required types and/or amounts of insurance
- Required professional licenses, software, equipment, storage, or space
- Required subconsultant percentages
- Statements on conflicts of interest
- Terms that limit or impact earnings or gross margins
- Unassigned liability or risk

While some of these items are clear problems that will need to be addressed (such as unclear language or undefined expectations) other items (such as the contract type) are simply important to be aware of because they may impact how you approach the project.

5.4 Perform Contract Negotiations

This is one of the many places where a good relationship with your client truly pays off. Relationships offer the opportunity to discuss and influence the terms and conditions of a project before you are awarded a contract. Strong relationships also make it easier to negotiate fair contract terms. This is why, during BD efforts, it is important to get to know the people in your client's organization who are involved in contracting and negotiations. Understanding how a client typically approaches the negotiation process makes it easier for you to suggest an alternative to a less-than-ideal contract term.

Plan negotiation rehearsals so that your firm representatives are all on the same page when they walk into the room—each person should know who manages which part of the discussion and when it is appropriate to ask questions or interject comments.

IDEA

Consider engaging legal, risk management, and financial advisors during contract negotiations to help you develop policies and processes that will protect your firm from risk while retaining a positive relationship with your client. A large firm may have such experts on staff full time, while smaller firms may hire them on retainer.

5.4.1 Mitigate Risks

The assessment of risk starts early in the pursuit process and continues through the life of the project. The amount of risk present at any given time will affect discussions on pricing and the allocation of responsibility for shouldering that risk. Therefore, each risk should be evaluated based on its potential impact on your firm. Consider:

- How likely is this risk to occur?
- What is the cost to your firm if the risk does occur?
- When would the risk likely occur (at what point in the pursuit or delivery timeline)?
- What is your strategy for dealing with that risk? Will you avoid, transfer, mitigate, or accept the risk?
- Who is responsible for monitoring that risk? How? When?

The goal is to figure out a way to accommodate risk in the contract so that both your firm and the client carry a reasonable amount.

TARGET POINT
Clearing the Land

Carstairs Construction Co. made the winning bid to build a shopping center on land that had, until recently, been a dairy farm. None of the late farmer's heirs was interested in continuing on the land, and a development company had put out an RFP for exactly the kind of work that Carstairs had been successful in for the past decade.

The owner of Carstairs was not only an experienced builder; she was also a long-time resident of the area, and well-acquainted with the ways that land can be tied up in a farming community. During contract negotiations, she stipulated that any costs associated with clearing the title to the land would be borne by the development company, including any work done that could not be completed due to problems with ownership.

With this understanding, Carstairs went ahead with a preliminary design for the project. After a few weeks, however, the developers found themselves in the middle of a lawsuit over who owned a significant part of the property, and they called a halt to further work.

Based on the contract, Carstairs was able to get reimbursement for their design work; and, while they didn't realize the profits that they had hoped for, they weren't out of pocket for the work that they had performed.

Key Concepts for this Story:
- A contract is designed to mitigate risk of non-performance by one party or the other.
- Exposure to a specific type of risk, such as unclear title, can be guarded against by a clearly worded contractual agreement.
- Different types of projects carry different risks that must be accounted for in the contract.

Make sure that the contract includes terms that help mitigate any risks associated with performing the project. Consider including the following:

- **Ownership and use of documents.** Confirm that your firm's drawings, specifications, and other documents, including those in electronic form, are to be used solely for the project at issue. The architect and any consultants should be identified as the authors and owners of the documents and retain all rights, including copyrights, to those documents. The issue of whether the design professional grants a non-exclusive license to reproduce the documents to the owner may be considered.

- **Waiver of consequential damages.** Consequential damages are those damages that are not directly caused by a breach of contract, but may result from it. The waiver should be clear and specify the kinds of consequential damages

considered to be waived, including home office overhead, loss of profits, and the like.

- **Limitation of liability.** Include a provision that defines and limits the types and amounts of damages for which you can be held responsible. In a best-case scenario, this provision should specifically state the maximum dollar amount of your liability for all professional obligations that you have agreed in the contract to undertake.

- **Termination of services.** Make sure that the agreement clearly defines under what circumstances the owner/client or the design professional may terminate the services. Particularly important is whether the services may be terminated at will (i.e., for convenience) and, if so, what compensation shall be due to you under that circumstance. In addition, notice requirements should be included in the agreement, indicating what notice must be given prior to termination. The agreement may also contain provisions as to what constitutes termination for cause. Those matters should be specifically identified, and, again, language should be included as to what constitutes the basis for a "for cause" termination.

5.4.2 Identify Negotiable vs Non-Negotiable Items

Identify which items are negotiable and which are not. Know what it is that you want to receive, what you are willing to settle for, and what you will walk away from. It is better to walk away from a risky scenario than to power through it, hoping for later change.

Determine your position on the budget, schedule, insurance, profit, overhead, markups on subconsultants, reimbursable items, other direct costs (ODC), wage and salary escalation, mobilization, and retainage. Every project should also have a contingency fee built into the contract to account for unknowns. This fee is basically an emergency fund—it's there to cover any delays, changes to regulations that affect the project scope, or other unexpected expenses that arise during the course of the project. Take into account how much you know about the project and how complete the plans for it are when negotiating contingencies. The more information you have, the smaller this fee should be, and vice versa.

5.4.3 Determine Participants

Find out who in the client's organization will lead the contracting effort, and who wields influence over the contracting process or timeline. Consider matching your negotiating team to their participants, level for level.

It's best for the people who participate in contract negotiations to not be emotionally attached to the project. However, do include the project manager or pursuit champion. A member of your leadership team, a business manager, or an operations officer may also be good participants. Some firms use the BD team to negotiate because they have the best relationship with the client, while others prefer to use the operations team because they are the ones responsible for performance and delivery. In still other firms, the firm partner or principal is almost always the person who conducts negotiations. Choose whether or not you want to reserve senior management for escalation purposes, should that need arise.

Consider including the following people:

- Someone who can capture notes and someone who can run numbers
- Experts who understand your firm's position on risk assessment, contracting and claims, and cash flow
- People whose personalities match those on your client's negotiations team

5.4.4 Collaborate

The ultimate goal of a negotiation session is to develop a contract that represents the best interests of both parties. Recognize that this is a win/win effort by starting the session with an agreement as to what the most positive outcome looks like. Eradicate any hidden agendas so that open communication can occur. Listen attentively to what the client wants—identify any points of pain that they are expressing and find a way to eliminate them.

It's always better to negotiate scope, rather than your fee. This respects the value of your work rather than commoditizing the service and focusing purely on cost. Consider trading items rather than reducing your fee. These items might include business referrals, a more relaxed schedule, changed payment terms or contract type, or intellectual property rights. Think: What items would the client consider to be of greatest benefit? You may be able to find an increased level of service or attention that they value, but that doesn't cost your firm much to provide.

5.5 Draft a Contract

The process of negotiating and drafting a contract helps your firm and the client to define and agree to the expectations for the project. It sets reference points for any necessary changes, performance issues, and dispute management. A good contract process ultimately reduces claims, increases profitability for both sides, and leads to high client satisfaction through the definition of the following basic elements:

- Scope of work. This provides the baseline for the project, and serves as the guide for all work going forward. It defines and quantifies all work-related activities, deliverables, and schedules. It also identifies applicable criteria, codes, and standards (including the date and edition) to be adhered to.
- Standard of care. This refers to the ordinary degree of skill and care that would be used by other reasonably competent practitioners of the same discipline under similar circumstances. Basically, it provides a framework for ascertaining whether your actions are reasonable, normal, and prudent under the given circumstances. When developing this section, avoid using superlatives that raise the standard of

care above what you can reasonably provide. For example: "We will provide the highest level of service."

TARGET POINT

Industry organizations have standard contract documents that many firms use as a foundation for their customized contract. These standard form contracts are issued by the AIA, the Design-Build Institute of America (DBIA), the Engineers Joint Contract Documents Committee (EJCDC), and Associated General Contractors (AGC). Use whichever contract best serves your purposes.

5.5.1 Understand the Difference in Contracts between Different Delivery Models

The four predominant models of project delivery—design-build (DB), design-bid-build (DBB), construction management at risk (CMAR), and AIA's integrated project delivery (IPD)—are largely defined by their contracting processes.

CMAR is a delivery model in which the owner establishes two contracts: one between the owner and designer, and one between the owner and builder. In this respect, CMAR emulates DBB: a dual-contract operation with which most owners are familiar and comfortable. However, CMAR differs from DBB in that the owner establishes these two contracts at about the same time, thereby allowing the builder to provide constructability input during the design process. With CMAR, the owner's A/E selection process is typically qualifications-based (as is the case with DBB), measuring the A/E's experience, past performance, capacity, and skills.

Since the drawings and specifications are incomplete when the owner initiates the two contracts, selection of the builder is not based on bid price (as is usually the case with DBB). The owner using the CMAR process usually evaluates the builder on qualification-based criteria in addition to cost factors. Qualification criteria usually include experience, past performance, capacity, financial strength, etc. One of the most notable advantages to CMAR for the owner is that builder selection is based on criteria other than simply lowest price.

From the owner's overall perspective, CMAR allows the designer and builder to collaborate with the owner from the project's beginning. The owner, designer, and builder can jointly evolve the solution, balancing the impacts of scope, cost, and schedule. This joint evolution lays the foundation for a spirit of teaming, shared responsibility, and tighter coordination of a project's details.

DB goes one step further in the integration of project team members by joining the designer and builder under a single contract with the owner. This single contract approach is what separates DB from DBB and CMAR. The collaborative advantages created in CMAR for the owner are reinforced in DB by use of a single contract. Since the designer and builder are "contractually" a single entity, the owner does not need to settle any disputes between the two. This particular DB feature is a significant expectation and selling point for owners: a single-point of accountability, responsibility, and administration.

As with CMAR, the owner can use non-price factors in the evaluation and selection of the design-builder: including experience, past performance, skills, capacity, management approach, and so on. These non-price factors can be combined with price factors (such as total price, unit cost, time/materials, etc.).

IPD is an integrated delivery model that maximizes the integration of the primary players on a project: namely the owner, designer, and builder. Collectively, these three form a "project entity"; one in which, for all intents and purposes, all have an ownership position. Developed by the AIA, IPD can be the ultimate "integrated" alternative delivery model. Since the owner, designer, and builder are members of a joint venture, their motivations are directed toward the project outcome rather than their individual positions. With IPD in general, all three players are partnered in their success or failure.

Because of the joint ownership position necessitated by the IPD model, public entities (such as government owners) are barred from such joint venture models. Private owners, however, are not prevented by any arrangement related to establishing a joint venture.

5.5.2 Understand the Differences in Contract Relationships

So far we have discussed only how to develop a prime contract—the contract between the lead firm on a project and the project's owner. But agreements and contracts drawn up between team members and partnered firms will differ from that type. Here are some of the other types of contract relationships that you may encounter:

- **Intent to team (or, teaming agreement).** This contract commits a firm to a team relationship, with expectations that the firm will support the team throughout the pursuit. It outlines reasons for which the agreement can be voided, and includes a general proposed scope of work.
- **Memorandum of understanding.** This outlines a common agreement between two firms to move forward prior to entering into a contract.
- **Subcontract.** A contract between a prime, or lead, firm and a firm being engaged for specific services or products.
- **Joint venture.** Agreements and contracts between firms that will share risk and responsibility as a contracting entity.

5.6 Sign the Contract

Make sure that firm leadership is aware of the contract provisions throughout negotiations; and have someone who is well-versed in legal, risk, and financial implications conduct a final review of the completed document. Also perform a detailed review and back-check of any changes made during negotiations—be especially aware of any penalty or incentive clauses.

The person who signs the contract must be someone with the legal authority to commit the firm to a contractual agreement. This usually requires holding Power of Attorney (POA) privileges, which often requires filing papers with government agencies.

Hold an AAR with the negotiating team to capture process improvements, best practices, and lessons learned for the next negotiation opportunity.

 ## 5.7 Key Terms

Below are the main terms covered in this section:

- Debriefing interview
- After action review (AAR)
- Net profit ratio
- Lump sum
- Cost plus
- Cost plus fixed fee
- Consequential damages
- Design-build (DB)
- Design-bid-build (DBB)
- Construction management at risk (CMAR)
- Integrated project delivery (IPD)

6   Case Study Activity

This Case Study Activity allows you to reflect on and apply the key concepts that you learned in this Domain to a real-world scenario. Each Domain includes a scenario about the same organization, Gilmore & Associates. The scenario is presented to you, followed by several questions. You can also elect to view the recommended solutions/responses for each question posed, which are located on the next page.

This case study can be used in many ways:

- You can individually reflect on the questions after reading the scenario, and write your own notes/responses to each question. You can then check your ability to apply the key concepts against the recommended solutions/responses.

- You can pull together a small group and use this scenario to drive a discussion around the challenge and to discuss solutions as a group.

- You can combine a selection of the case study activities (across the Domains) into a larger scenario-based activity as a part of a professional development event.

Gilmore & Associates, the mid-sized engineering firm you work for, has been presented with a game-changing opportunity. You've recently been leading the effort to transition your firm away from working primarily in the education sector, and towards healthcare projects that serve the growing retiree community in the area. One of the prospective clients that your team has been building a relationship with has just mentioned a new project that they will be embarking on in the upcoming year—a retirement community with a built-in rehabilitation facility that caters specifically to the needs of older adults.

This project is perfectly in line with your firm's strategic objectives, and the CEO is excited to go after it. It doesn't take long for your decision team to reach a "go" decision. Knowing about this project early on gives you plenty of time to develop a winning proposal.

1. Since your firm hasn't worked on many healthcare projects before, you are considering forming a partnership with a more experienced firm to improve your chances of winning the project. What factors should you consider when evaluating a firm as a potential partner?

2. The client releases the RFP, and the convoluted structure of the document makes it difficult to parse out what, precisely, is being requested. How can you ensure that you fully comprehend and meet all of the proposal requirements?

3. What can you do to make your proposal stand out?

4. You are informed that your project team has made the short list. You and two other firms have been invited to present on how your design for the retirement facility will best meet the client's needs. What can you do to prepare for the upcoming presentation and interview?

5. Your hard work has been rewarded—your firm won the project! How can you make the most of the debriefing session to help you relive this success in future proposals?

Answer Key

1. Since your firm hasn't worked on many healthcare projects before, you are considering forming a partnership with a more experienced firm to improve your chances of winning the project. What factors should you consider when evaluating a firm as a potential partner?

    o   Compare the skills and expertise required by the client against your firm's ability to provide them. Would a potential partner be able to fill in the gaps?

    o   Evaluate the strength of your relationship with the client. Do you have ties with the decision makers in the client's firm? Would your proposal benefit by partnering with a firm that knows the client better?

    o   Consider the culture of the firm that you're thinking about teaming with. Is it compatible with your own firm's culture, or will it require a major adjustment? Do your teams get along?

    o   Does the client have participation goals for SDBE firms?

2. The client releases the RFP, and the convoluted structure of the document makes it difficult to parse out what, precisely, is being requested. How can you ensure that you fully comprehend and meet all of the proposal requirements?

    o   Use a compliance matrix to deconstruct the RFP and reorganize it so that related information is grouped together.

    o   Develop questions and submit any requests for clarification to your point of contact in the client's firm.

    o   Find out if the questions and answers will be posted publically for your competitors to see.

    o   Ask your BD team what they know about the client's hot buttons. This information can be used to figure out their unstated requirements.

    o   Create a detailed work plan, complete with a schedule for tracking proposal elements and assigning responsibilities, so that none of the proposal requirements are ignored.

3. What can you do to make your proposal stand out?

    o   Build your proposal around a unifying theme that highlights the differentiators that your firm has that will most benefit your client.

- Tell a story, through examples and statistics, of how your team has provided value for similar projects in the past. Use text and graphics to create an engaging narrative. For example, the ways in which your experience designing K-12 schools have prepared you for designing this similarly-sized retirement facility.

- Think about why each project team member was selected and highlight their expertise.

- Keep the focus on your client—how your firm will address their worries, hopes, and needs.

4. You are informed that your project team has made the short list. You and two other firms have been invited to present on how your design for the retirement facility will best meet the client's needs. What can you do to prepare for the upcoming presentation and interview?

- Find out from your BD team what the client is looking for in the presentation. Identify and address their concerns with solutions that differentiate you from your competition.

- Visit the presentation space, if possible, or ask to see a picture of it so that you know what to expect on the day of the interview.

- Develop a storyboard to outline the presentation and ensure that all elements—salient points, graphics, narrative, etc.—flow together.

- Make sure that you have a contingency plan for anything that might go wrong, including technological difficulties.

- Rehearse the entire presentation at least three times, until all of your speakers can present their material conversationally and without notes.

5. Your hard work has been rewarded—your firm won the project! How can you make the most of the debriefing session to help you relive this success in future proposals?

- Develop open-ended questions that encourage the client to talk freely. Consider the debrief a conversation, rather than a formal interview.

- Find out what aspects of your proposal and interview that the client likes the most, and the least.

- Ask for any recommendations that they have for your future submittals.

- Find out if there are any other RFP opportunities in the near future that your firm might apply for.

7   Glossary

After Action Review (AAR)
An open dialogue with the people involved in the project pursuit and conducted before a formal debrief session is held with the client.

Blue Team Review
The initial review of a proposal, used to select résumés and project descriptions, and to evaluate the availability of required content.

Boilerplate
Standardized statements about an organization, its operations, or business philosophy. Examples include firm history, mission statement, vision statement, QC procedures, executive team, financial status, service descriptions, typical RFP topic responses, etc.

Compliance Matrix
A tool used to ensure that a proposal complies with all of the requirements detailed in an RFP. The matrix allows the content of the RFP to be deconstructed and reorganized so that related information is placed together.

Consequential Damages
Damages that are not directly caused by one party's breach of a contract, but which may result from the breach. Legal principles allow for parties to a contract to agree to waive their right to collect these types of damages in the event of a breach.

Construction Management at Risk (CMAR)
A form of project delivery that entails a commitment by the construction manager to deliver the project within a guaranteed maximum price (GMP), in most cases. The construction manager acts as consultant to the owner in the development and design phases but as the equivalent of a general contractor during the construction phase.

Cost Plus
A fee structure where the design professional agrees to provide services at cost plus a multiplier.

Cost Plus Fixed Fee
A fee structure where the design professional agrees to provide services with reimbursement at a standard overhead rate with a standard profit percentage.

Debriefing Interview
A meeting between a firm and its (prospective) client to discuss a winning/losing proposal. The debrief helps businesses better understand their clients' needs and provides information that can be used to improve marketing efforts.

Design-Bid-Build (DBB)
A form of project delivery whereby the contracting agency either performs the design work in-house or negotiates with an engineering design firm to prepare drawings and specifications under a design services contract, and then separately contracts for at risk construction by engaging a contractor through competitive bidding. This is the traditional delivery methodology used by most public agencies.

Design-Build (DB)

A form of project delivery whereby one entity (one company or two or more companies in a teaming arrangement) performs both architectural/engineering and construction under one single contract. Under this arrangement, the design-builder warrants to the contracting agency that it will produce design documents that are complete and free from error (design-builder takes the risk).

Go/No-Go Process

Thought process or checklist to analyze whether or not it is worth expending manpower and financial resources to pursue a particular project; some are more formal than others.

Integrated Project Delivery (IPD)

A project delivery approach that integrates people, systems, business structures, and practices into a process that collaboratively harnesses the talents and insights of all participants to reduce waste and optimize efficiency through all phases of design, fabrication, and construction.

Long Lead Items

Activities on a schedule that typically require a longer time to acquire or complete, and therefore need to be started earlier than other items.

Lump Sum

A fee structure where the design professional determines a fixed fee under which they agree to deliver a specific scope of work.

Minority-Owned Business Enterprise (MBE)

A firm that government agencies recognize as being at least 51 percent owned and controlled by individuals of African-American, Asian, Hispanic, or Native American ethnicity.

Net Profit Ratio

The ratio of net profit (income minus expenses) to net revenues.

Proposal

Document prepared in response to a specific solicitation where generally the project is identified and a scope of work is available. Includes general firm information, relevant projects, a technical project understanding/approach, and key staff résumés.

Quality Assurance (QA)

Activities related to the production of a quality product or service.

Quality Control (QC)

Activities that review finished products or current service lines to ensure that they meet established quality requirements.

Red Team Review

The primary review of a proposal—offers a chance for a team to catch errors or omissions before the proposal is submitted.

Request for Information (RFI)

Generally comes from a team member requiring additional information or clarification from a party, for example, a contractor requesting information on a detail from the architect.

Request for Proposal (RFP)

Document used in procurement procedures through which a purchaser advises potential suppliers of (1) description of goods and/or services to be procured; (2) technical goals; (3) statement and scope of work; (4) specifications; (5) schedules or timelines; (6) general criteria used in evaluation procedure; (7) contract type; (8) terms and conditions; (9) special contractual requirements; (10) data requirements; and (11) instructions for preparation of technical, management, and/or cost proposals.

Request for Qualifications (RFQ)

A procurement tool routinely used to narrow interested partners for further consideration. In the A/E/C industry, an RFQ may be used to pre-qualify firms for a specific task (architecture, engineering, or construction) or project. An RFQ is often followed by an RFP requesting more detailed information to assist the owner in selecting the preferred partner for a project. A Statement of Qualifications (SOQ) is the typical response to an RFQ.

SDBE (Small Disadvantaged Business Enterprise)

A firm that government agencies recognize as having annual revenues below a designated level and at least 51 percent owned and controlled by members of a disadvantaged population.

Short List

List of firms generated once responses to an RFQ or RFP have been submitted and reviewed by the client. Short-listed firms are given the opportunity to continue through the procurement process by submitting a proposal and/or giving a presentation to the client. From the short list, one firm will ultimately be selected to negotiate a contract and perform the work.

Standard Form 255/254 (SF 255/254)

An older version of the SF 330 that is still used by some non-Federal agencies.

Standard Form 330 (SF 330)

The standard form used by Federal agencies in the procurement of architecture and engineering services.

Statement of Qualifications (SOQ)

Document prepared as a more general response for a client, soliciting qualified firms for a specific area of practice or project. Usually includes general firm information and relevant projects, and may include information on proposed key staff. It may include a project understanding, but generally does not include a technical project approach.

Storyboard (presentation)

A form of graphic organization that uses illustrations, images, or pages displayed in sequence for the purpose of pre-visualizing a presentation.

Women-Owned Business Enterprise (WBE)
A firm that government agencies recognize as being at least 51 percent owned and controlled by women.

Work Plan
A written plan that defines action, which typically includes tactics, timetable, individuals responsible, and results accomplished.

8   Related Resources

SF 330 Form and Instructions:

    www.gsa.gov/forms

FedBizOpps Website:

    www.fbo.gov

9   Figures

10   Index

W

11   About the Photographer:

Paul Turang is an award-winning photographer who has been photographing architecture and design-related projects for nearly 20 years. Turang and his team have photographed projects throughout the nation. His images have received several international awards and have been featured in a variety of design related publications, including Architectural Record; Buildings: Healthcare Design, Hospitality and Design; Interiors and Sources; Metropolis; LD+A; and others. A member of SMPS Los Angeles, Turang travels regularly for assignments, bringing his passion and vision to leading architecture, design, and construction firms. His website is http://paulturang.com and he can be contacted at paul@paulturang.com.

12   Peer Review:

The following professionals have peer reviewed one or more domains of the MARKENDIUM: The SMPS Body of Knowledge.

Ed Hannan, Executive Editor

Janet Brooks, CPSM
Cynthia Jackson, FSMPS, CPSM
Francis Lippert, FSMPS, CPSM
Fawn Radmanich, CPSM
Julie Shepard, CPSM, ENV SP
Andrea Story, CPSM

13 Body of Knowledge Subject Matter Experts (SMEs)

Dana L. Birkes, APR, FSMPS, CPSM

CMO, Clifford Power Systems, Tulsa, OK

Scott W. Braley, FAIA, FRSA

Principal Consultant, Braley Consulting & Training, Atlanta, GA

Theresa M. Casey, FSMPS, CPSM

Principal, On Target Marketing & Communications LLC, Columbia, CT

Karen O. Courtney, AIA, FSMPS

Chief Marketing Officer, Fanning Howey, Indianapolis, IN

Dana Galvin Lancour, FSMPS, CPSM

Director of Communications, Barton Malow Company, Southfield, MI

Shannah A. Hayley, FSMPS, CPSM

Director of Marketing and Community Engagement, City of Plano, Plano, TX

Linda M. Koch, FSMPS, CPSM

Director of Marketing & Business Development, Pfluger Architects, San Antonio, TX

Michael J. Reilly, FSMPS

Principal, Reilly Communications, Boston, MA

Laurie B. Strickland, FSMPS, CPSM

Director of Marketing, Nitsch Engineering, Boston, MA

Mark Tawara, FSMPS, CPSM

Owner, Manageability, LLC, Kailua, HI

Nancy J. Usrey, FSMPS, CPSM

Associate Vice President, HNTB Design Build, Plano, TX

Andrew J. Weinberg, FSMPS, CPSM

Regional Business Development Manager, Simpson Gumpertz & Heger Inc., New York, NY

Made in the USA
Middletown, DE
20 March 2019